PLACE Basic Skills
090 Teacher Certification Exam

By: Sharon Wynne, M.S
Southern Connecticut State University

"And, while there's no reason yet to panic, I think it's only prudent that we make preparations to panic."

XAMonline, INC.
Boston

Copyright © 2007 XAMonline, Inc.
All rights reserved. No part of the material protected by this copyright notice may be reproduced or utilized in any form or by any means, electronic or mechanical, including photocopying, recording or by any information storage and retrievable system, without written permission from the copyright holder.

To obtain permission(s) to use the material from this work for any purpose including workshops or seminars, please submit a written request to:

> XAMonline, Inc.
> 21 Orient Ave.
> Melrose, MA 02176
> Toll Free 1-800-509-4128
> Email: info@xamonline.com
> Web www.xamonline.com
> Fax: 1-781-662-9268

Library of Congress Cataloging-in-Publication Data

Wynne, Sharon A.
    Basic Skills 90: Teacher Certification / Sharon A. Wynne. -2nd ed.
    ISBN 978-1-58197-768-4
        1. Basic Skills 90   2. Study Guides.   3. PLACE
        4. Teachers' Certification & Licensure.   5. Careers

Disclaimer:
The opinions expressed in this publication are the sole works of XAMonline and were created independently from the National Education Association, Educational Testing Service, or any State Department of Education, National Evaluation Systems or other testing affiliates.

Between the time of publication and printing, state specific standards, testing formats, and website information may change. Any such changes are not addressed in part or in whole within this product. Sample test questions are developed by XAMonline and reflect content similar to that appearing on real tests; however, they are not former tests. XAMonline assembles content that aligns with state standards, but it does not guarantee that teacher candidates will achieve a passing score . Numerical scores are determined by testing companies such as NES or ETS and then are compared with individual state standards. A passing score varies from state to state.

Printed in the United States of America   œ-1

PLACE: Basic Skills 90
ISBN: 978-1-58197-768-4

TEACHER CERTIFICATION STUDY GUIDE

Table of Contents

DOMAIN I.   **MATHEMATICS**

COMPETENCY 1.0   **KNOWLEDGE OF NUMBER SENSE, CONCEPTS AND OPERATIONS** 1

Skill 1.1   Compare the relative value of real numbers 1

Skill 1.2   Solve real-world problems involving addition, subtraction, multiplication, and division of rational numbers 4

Skill 1.3   Apply basic number theory concepts including the use of primes, composites, factors, and multiples in solving problems 18

Skill 1.4   Apply the order of operations with or without grouping symbols 20

COMPETENCY 2.0   **KNOWLEDGE OF MEASUREMENT** 21

Skill 2.1   Solve real-world problems involving length, weight, mass, perimeter, area, capacity, and volume 21

Skill 2.2   Solve real-world problems involving rated measures 29

Skill 2.3   Solve real-world problems involving scaled drawings 31

Skill 2.4   Solve real-world problems involving the change of units of measures of length, weight, mass, capacity, and time 31

Skill 2.5   Solve real-world problems involving estimates of measures including length, weight, mass, temperature, time, money, perimeter, area, and volume 33

Skill 2.6   Choose the correct reading, to a specified degree of accuracy, using instruments 37

BASIC SKILLS

TEACHER CERTIFICATION STUDY GUIDE

COMPETENCY 3.0 KNOWLEDGE OF GEOMETRY AND SPATIAL SENSE 39

Skill 3.1 Identify and/or classify simple two-and three-dimensional figures according to their properties 39

Skill 3.2 Solve real-world and mathematical problems involving ratio, proportion, similarity, congruence, and the Pythagorean relationship 43

Skill 3.3 Identify the location of ordered pairs of integers in all four quadrants of a coordinate system and use the coordinate system to apply the concepts of slope and distance to solve problems 50

Skill 3.4 Identify real-world examples that represent geometric concepts including perpendicularity, parallelism, tangency, symmetry, and transformations 52

COMPETENCY 4.0 KNOWLEDGE OF ALGEBRAIC THINKING 56

Skill 4.1 Analyze and generalize patterns including arithmetic and geometric sequences 56

Skill 4.2 Interpret algebraic expressions using words, symbols, variables, tables, and graphs 57

Skill 4.3 Solve equations and inequalities graphically or algebraically 59

Skill 4.4 Determine whether a number or ordered pair is among the solutions of given equations or inequalities 73

BASIC SKILLS

TEACHER CERTIFICATION STUDY GUIDE

COMPETENCY 5.0 KNOWLEDGE OF DATA ANALYSIS AND PROBABILITY 74

Skill 5.1 Analyze data and solve problems using data presented in histograms, bar graphs, circle graphs, pictographs, tables, and charts 74

Skill 5.2 Identify how the presentation of data can lead to different or inappropriate interpretations 77

Skill 5.3 Calculate range, mean, median, and mode(s) from sets of data and interpret the meaning of the measures of central tendency and dispersion 77

Skill 5.4 Identify how the measures of central tendency can lead to different interpretations 79

Skill 5.5 Calculate the probability of a specified outcome 80

Skill 5.6 Solve and interpret real-world problems involving probability using counting procedures, tables, tree diagrams, and the concepts of permutations and combination 83

Sample Test: Mathematics 90

Answer Key: Mathematics 104

Rationales for Sample Questions: Mathematics 105

BASIC SKILLS

TEACHER CERTIFICATION STUDY GUIDE

DOMAIN II.   **ENGLISH**

COMPETENCY 6.0   CONCEPTUAL AND ORGANIZATIONAL SKILLS 111

Skill 6.1   Identify logical order in a written passage 111

Skill 6.2   Identify irrelevant sentences 113

COMPETENCY 7.0   WORD CHOICE SKILLS 115

Skill 7.1   Choose the appropriate word or expression in context 115

Skill 7.2   Recognize commonly confused or misused words or phrases 120

Skill 7.3   Recognize diction and tone appropriate to a given audience 124

COMPETENCY 8.0   SENTENCE STRUCTURE SKILLS 126

Skill 8.1   Recognize correct placement of modifiers 126

Skill 8.2   Recognize parallelism, including parallel expressions for parallel ideas 130

Skill 8.3   Recognize fragments, comma splices, and run-on sentences 134

TEACHER CERTIFICATION STUDY GUIDE

COMPETENCY 9.0 GRAMMAR, SPELLING, CAPITALIZATION, AND PUNCTUATION SKILLS 141

Skill 9.1 Identify standard verb forms 141

Skill 9.2 Identify inappropriate shifts in verb tense 145

Skill 9.3 Identify agreement between subject and verb 148

Skill 9.4 Identify agreement between pronoun and antecedent 151

Skill 9.5 Identify inappropriate pronoun shifts 154

Skill 9.6 Identify clear pronoun references 155

Skill 9.7 Identify proper case forms 156

Skill 9.8 Identify the correct use of adjectives and adverbs 160

Skill 9.9 Identify appropriate comparative and superlative degree forms 163

Skill 9.10 Identify standard spelling 166

Skill 9.11 Identify standard punctuation 169

Skill 9.12 Identify standard capitalization 174

Sample Test: English 179

Answer Key: English 190

Rationales for Sample Questions: English 191

TEACHER CERTIFICATION STUDY GUIDE

DOMAIN III. READING

COMPETENCY 10.0 KNOWLEDGE LITERAL COMPREHENSION 197

    Skill 10.1   Recognize main ideas 197

    Skill 10.2   Identify supporting details 198

    Skill 10.3   Determine the meaning of words or phrases in context 199

COMPETENCY 11.0 KNOWLEDGE OF INFERENTIAL COMPREHENSION 204

    Skill 11.1   Determine purpose 204

    Skill 11.2   Identify overall organizational pattern 206

    Skill 11.3   Distinguish between fact and opinion 207

    Skill 11.4   Recognize bias 208

    Skill 11.5   Recognize tone 209

    Skill 11.6   Recognize relationships between sentences 210

    Skill 11.7   Analyze the validity of arguments 211

    Skill 11.8   Draw logical inferences and conclusion 212

Sample Test: Reading 215

Answer Key: Reading 222

Rationales for Sample Questions: Reading 223

TEACHER CERTIFICATION STUDY GUIDE

DOMAIN IV. ESSAY

COMPETENCY 12.0   ESSAY 226

Skill 12.1   Determine the purpose for writing 227

Skill 12.2   Formulate a thesis or statement of main idea 228

Skill 12.3   Organize ideas and details effectively 233

Skill 12.4   Provide adequate, relevant supporting material 236

Skill 12.5   Use effective transitions 236

Skill 12.6   Demonstrate a mature command of language 236

Skill 12.7   Avoid inappropriate use of slang, jargon and clichés 236

Skill 12.8   Use a variety of sentence patterns effectively 236

Skill 12.9   Maintain consistent point of view... 237

Skill 12.10 Observe the conventions of standard American English............ 237

Great Study and Testing Tips!

What to study in order to prepare for the subject assessments is the focus of this study guide, but equally important is *how* you study.

You can increase your chances of truly mastering the information by taking some simple, but effective, steps.

Study Tips:

1. Some foods aid the learning process. Foods such as milk, nuts, seeds, rice, and oats help your study efforts by releasing natural memory enhancers called CCKs (*cholecystokinin*) composed of *tryptopha*n, *choline*, and *phenylalanine*. All of these chemicals enhance the neurotransmitters associated with memory. Before studying, try a light, protein-rich meal of eggs, turkey, and fish. All of these foods release the memory-enhancing chemicals. The better the connections, the more you comprehend.

Likewise, before you take a test, stick to a light snack of energy-boosting and relaxing foods. A glass of milk, a piece of fruit, or some peanuts all release various memory-boosting chemicals and help you to relax and focus on the subject at hand.

2. Learn to take great notes. A by-product of our modern culture is that we have grown accustomed to getting our information in short doses (i.e. TV news sound bites or USA Today style newspaper articles.)

Consequently, we've subconsciously trained ourselves to assimilate information better in neat little packages. If your notes are scrawled all over the paper, it fragments the flow of the information. Strive for clarity. Newspapers use a standard format to achieve clarity. Your notes can be much clearer through use of proper formatting. A very effective format is called the *"Cornell Method."*

> Take a sheet of loose-leaf lined notebook paper and draw a line all the way down the paper about 1-2" from the left-hand edge.
>
> Draw another line across the width of the paper about 1-2" up from the bottom. Repeat this process on the reverse side of the page.

Look at the highly effective result. You have ample room for notes, a left hand margin for special emphasis items or inserting supplementary data from the textbook, a large area at the bottom for a brief summary, and a little rectangular space for just about anything you want.

3. **Get the concept, then the details.** Too often we focus on the details and don't gather an understanding of the concept. However, if you simply memorize only dates, places, or names, you may well miss the whole point of the subject.

A key way to understand things is to put them in your own words. If you are working from a textbook, automatically summarize each paragraph in your mind. If you are outlining text, don't simply copy the author's words.

Rephrase them in your own words. This is known as paraphrasing. You remember your own thoughts and words much better than someone else's, and subconsciously tend to associate the important details to the core concepts.

4. **Ask Why?** Pull apart written material paragraph by paragraph, and don't forget the captions under the illustrations.

Example: If the heading is "Stream Erosion", flip it around to read "Why do streams erode?" Then answer the questions.

If you train your mind to think in a series of questions and answers, not only will you learn more, but you will also experience less test anxiety because you are used to answering questions.

5. **Read for reinforcement and future needs.** Even if you only have 10 minutes, put your notes or a book in your hand. Your mind is similar to a computer; you have to input data in order to have it processed. *By reading, you are creating neural connections for future retrieval.* The more times you read something, the more you reinforce the learning of ideas.

Even if you don't fully understand something on the first pass, *your mind stores much of the material for later recall.*

6. **Relax to learn so, go into exile.** Our bodies respond to an inner clock based on biorhythms. Burning the midnight oil works well for some people, but not for everyone.

If possible, set aside a particular place to study that is free of distractions. Shut off the television, cell phone, and pager; and exile your friends and family during your study period.

If you really are bothered by silence, try background music. Light classical music at a low volume has been shown to aid in concentration over other types. Music that evokes pleasant emotions without lyrics are highly suggested. Try just about anything by Mozart. It relaxes you.

7. **Use arrows, not highlighters.** At best, it's difficult to read a page full of yellow, pink, blue, and green streaks. Try staring at a neon sign for a while, and you'll soon see that the horde of colors obscures the message.

A quick note, a brief dash of color, an underline, and an arrow pointing to a particular passage is much clearer than a horde of highlighted words.

8. **Budget your study time.** Although you shouldn't ignore any of the material, *allocate your available study time in the same ratio that topics are likely to appear on the test.*

TEACHER CERTIFICATION STUDY GUIDE

Testing Tips:

1. <u>**Get smart, play dumb**</u>. **Don't read anything into the question.** Don't make an assumption that the test writer is looking for something else than what is asked. Stick to the question as written, and don't read extra things into it.

2. <u>**Read the question and all the choices *twice* before answering the question**</u>. You may miss something by not carefully reading, and then re-reading, both the question and the answers.

If you really don't have a clue as to the right answer, leave it blank on the first time through. Go on to the other questions because they may provide a clue as to how to answer the skipped questions.

If later on, you still can't answer the skipped ones . . . ***Guess.*** The only penalty for guessing is that you *might* get it wrong. Only one thing is certain; if you don't put anything down, you will get it wrong!

3. <u>**Turn the question into a statement**</u>. Look at the way the questions are worded. The syntax of the question usually provides a clue. Does it seem more familiar as a statement rather than as a question? Does it sound strange?

By turning a question into a statement, you may be able to spot if an answer sounds right, and it may also trigger memories of material you have read.

4. <u>**Look for hidden clues**</u>. It's actually very difficult to compose multiple-foil (choice) questions without giving away part of the answer in the options presented.

In most multiple-choice questions, you can often readily eliminate one or two of the potential answers. This leaves you with only two real possibilities, and automatically your odds go to Fifty-Fifty.

5. <u>**Trust your instincts**</u>. For every fact that you have read, you subconsciously retain something of that knowledge. On questions that you aren't really certain about, go with your basic instincts. **Your first impression on how to answer a question is usually correct.**

6. <u>**Mark your answers directly on the test booklet**</u>. Don't bother trying to fill in the optical scan sheet on the first pass through the test.

Be careful not to miss-mark your answers when you transcribe them to the scan sheet.

7. <u>**Watch the clock!**</u> You have a set amount of time to answer the questions. Don't get bogged down trying to answer a single question at the expense of ten questions you can more readily answer.

BASIC SKILLS

THIS PAGE BLANK

TEACHER CERTIFICATION STUDY GUIDE

DOMAIN I.   **MATHEMATICS**

COMPETENCY 1.0   **KNOWLEDGE OF NUMBER SENSE, CONCEPTS, AND OPERATIONS**

Skill 1.1   Compare the relative value of real numbers (e.g., integers, fractions, decimals, percents, irrational numbers, and numbers expressed in exponential or scientific notation).

We can express **rational numbers** as the ratio of two integers $\frac{a}{b}$, where $b \neq 0$. For example, $\frac{2}{3}$, $-\frac{4}{5}$, $5 = \frac{5}{1}$.

The rational numbers include integers, fractions, mixed numbers, and terminating and repeating decimals. We can express every rational number as a repeating or terminating decimal and represent it on a number line.

Integers are positive and negative whole numbers and zero.
    ...-6, -5, -4, -3, -2, -1, 0, 1, 2, 3, 4, 5, 6, ...

Whole numbers are natural numbers and zero.
    0, 1, 2, 3, ,4 ,5 ,6 ...

Natural numbers are the counting numbers.
    1, 2, 3, 4, 5, 6, ...

Irrational numbers are real numbers that we cannot be write as the ratio of two integers. These are infinite non-repeating decimals.
    Examples: $\sqrt{5} = 2.2360..$,   pi $=\prod= 3.1415927...$

A **fraction** is an expression of numbers in the form of x/y, where x is the numerator and y is the denominator, which cannot be zero.

Example: $\frac{3}{7}$ 3 is the numerator, 7 is the denominator

If the fraction has common factors for the numerator and denominator, divide both by the common factor to reduce the fraction to its lowest form.

Example:

$\frac{13}{39} = \frac{1 \times 13}{3 \times 13} = \frac{1}{3}$ Divide by the common factor 13

BASIC SKILLS

A **mixed** number has an integer part and a fractional part.

Example: $2\frac{1}{4}, \ ^-5\frac{1}{6}, \ 7\frac{1}{3}$

Percent = per 100 (written with the symbol %). Thus $10\% = \frac{10}{100} = \frac{1}{10}$.

Decimals = deci = part of ten. To find the decimal equivalent of a fraction, use the denominator to divide the numerator as shown in the following example.

Example: Find the decimal equivalent of $\frac{7}{10}$.

Since 10 cannot divide into 7 evenly

$\frac{7}{10} = 0.7$

The **exponent form** is a shortcut method to write repeated multiplication. Basic form: b^n, where b is the base and n is the exponent. b and n are both real numbers. b^n indicates that we multiply the base, b, by itself n times.

Examples: $3^4 = 3 \times 3 \times 3 \times 3 = 81$

$2^3 = 2 \times 2 \times 2 = 8$

$(^-2)^4 = (^-2) \times (^-2) \times (^-2) \times (^-2) = 16$

$^-2^4 = ^-(2 \times 2 \times 2 \times 2) = ^-16$

Key exponent rules:

For 'a' (nonzero), and 'm' and 'n' (real numbers):

1) $a^m \cdot a^n = a^{(m+n)}$ Product rule

2) $\dfrac{a^m}{a^n} = a^{(m-n)}$ Quotient rule

3) $\dfrac{a^{-m}}{a^{-n}} = \dfrac{a^n}{a^m}$

When we raise 10 to any power, the exponent tells us the number of zeroes in the product.

BASIC SKILLS

Example: $10^7 = 10,000,000$

Caution: Unless the negative sign is inside the parentheses and the exponent is outside the parentheses, the exponent does not affect the sign.

$(^-2)^4$ implies that we multiply -2 by itself 4 times.

$^-2^4$ implies that we multiply 2 by itself 4 times, then negate the answer.

Scientific notation is a more convenient method for writing very large and very small numbers. It employs two factors. The first factor is a number between 1 and 10. The second factor is a power of 10. This notation is a "shorthand" for expressing large numbers (like the weight of 100 elephants) or small numbers (like the weight of an atom in pounds).

Recall that:

$10^n = (10)^n$ Ten multiplied by itself n times.

$10^0 = 1$ Any nonzero number raised to power of zero is 1.
$10^1 = 10$
$10^2 = 10 \times 10 = 100$
$10^3 = 10 \times 10 \times 10 = 1000$ (kilo)
$10^{-1} = 1/10$ (deci)
$10^{-2} = 1/100$ (centi)
$10^{-3} = 1/1000$ (milli)
$10^{-6} = 1/1,000,000$ (micro)

Example: Write 46,368,000 in scientific notation.

1) Introduce a decimal point and decimal places.
   46,368,000 = 46,368,000.0000

2) Make a mark between the two digits that give a number between -9.9 and 9.9.
   4∧6,368,000.0000

3) Count the number of digit places between the decimal point and the ∧ mark. This number is the 'n'-the power of ten.

   So, $46,368,000 = 4.6368 \times 10^7$

BASIC SKILLS

Example: Write 0.00397 in scientific notation.

1) Decimal place is already in place.

2) Make a mark between 3 and 9 to form a number between -9.9 and 9.9.

3) Move decimal place to the mark (3 hops).

0.003 ∧ 97

Motion is to the right, so n of 10^n is negative.

Therefore, $0.00397 = 3.97 \times 10^{-3}$.

Skill 1.2 **Solve real-world problems involving addition, subtraction, multiplication, and division of rational numbers (e.g., whole numbers, integers, decimals, percents, and fractions including mixed numbers).**

Properties are rules that apply for addition, subtraction, multiplication, or division of real numbers. These properties are:

Commutative: You can change the order of the terms or factors as follows.

  For addition: $a + b = b + a$
  For multiplication: $ab = ba$

Associative: You can regroup the terms as you like.

  For addition: $a + (b + c) = (a + b) + c$
  For multiplication: $a(bc) = (ab)c$

This rule does not apply for division and subtraction.

Example: $(^-2 + 7) + 5 = ^-2 + (7 + 5)$
         $5 + 5 = ^-2 + 12 = 10$

Example: $(3 \times ^-7) \times 5 = 3 \times (^-7 \times 5)$
         $^-21 \times 5 = 3 \times ^-35 = ^-105$

Identity: A number that when added to a term results in that same number (additive identity); a number that when multiplied by a term results in that same number (multiplicative identity).

For addition: $a + 0 = a$ (zero is additive identity)
For multiplication: $a \times 1 = a$ (one is multiplicative)

Example: $17 + 0 = 17$

Example: $^-34 \times 1 = {^-34}$

The product of any number and one is that number.

Distributive: This technique allows us to operate on terms within a parentheses without first performing operations within the parentheses. This is especially helpful when we cannot combine terms within the parentheses.

$a(b + c) = ab + ac$

Example: $6 \times (^-4 + 9) = (6 \times {^-4}) + (6 \times 9)$
$6 \times 5 = {^-24} + 54 = 30$

To multiply a sum by a number, multiply each addend by the number, then add the products.

BASIC SKILLS

Addition of whole numbers

Example: At the end of a day of shopping, a shopper had $24 remaining in his wallet. He spent $45 on various goods. How much money did the shopper have at the beginning of the day?

The total amount of money the shopper started with is the sum of the amount spent and the amount remaining at the end of the day.

$$\begin{array}{r} 24 \\ +\ 45 \\ \hline 69 \end{array}$$ → The original total was $69.

Example: The winner of a race took 1 hr. 58 min. 12 sec. on the first half of the race and 2 hr. 9 min. 57 sec. on the second half of the race. What was the winner's total time?

```
  1 hr. 58 min. 12 sec.
+ 2 hr.  9 min. 57 sec.         Add these numbers
  3 hr. 67 min. 69 sec.
+       1 min - 60 sec.         Change 60 seconds to 1min.
  3 hr. 68 min.  9 sec.
+ 1 hr.-60 min.          .      Change 60 minutes to 1 hr.
  4 hr.  8 min.  9 sec.  ←  Final answer
```

Subtraction of Whole Numbers

Example: At the end of his shift, a cashier has $96 in the cash register. At the beginning of his shift, he had $15. How much money did the cashier collect during his shift?

The total collected is the difference of the ending amount and the starting amount.

$$\begin{array}{r} 96 \\ -\ 15 \\ \hline 81 \end{array}$$ → The total collected was $81.

BASIC SKILLS

TEACHER CERTIFICATION STUDY GUIDE

Multiplication of whole numbers

Multiplication is one of the four basic number operations. In simple terms, multiplication is the addition of a number to itself a certain number of times. For example, 4 multiplied by 3 is the equal to 4 + 4 + 4 or 3 + 3 + 3 +3. Another way of conceptualizing multiplication is to think in terms of groups. For example, if we have 4 groups of 3 students, the total number of students is 4 multiplied by 3. We call the solution to a multiplication problem the product.

The basic algorithm for whole number multiplication begins with aligning the numbers by place value with the number containing more places on top.

$$\begin{array}{r} 172 \\ \times\ 43 \end{array}$$ ⟶ Note that we placed 122 on top because it has more places than 43 has.

Next, we multiply the ones' place of the second number by each place value of the top number sequentially.

$$\begin{array}{r} (2) \\ 172 \\ \times\ 43 \\ \hline 516 \end{array}$$ ⟶ {3 x 2 = 6, 3 x 7 = 21, 3 x 1 = 3}
Note that we had to carry a 2 to the hundreds' column because 3 x 7 = 21. Note also that we add, not multiply, carried numbers to the product.

Next, we multiply the number in the tens' place of the second number by each place value of the top number sequentially. Because we are multiplying by a number in the tens' place, we place a zero at the end of this product.

$$\begin{array}{r} (2) \\ 172 \\ \times\ 43 \\ \hline 516 \\ 6880 \end{array}$$ ⟶ {4 x 2 = 8, 4 x 7 = 28, 4 x 1 = 4}

Finally, to determine the final product we add the two partial products.

$$\begin{array}{r} 172 \\ \times\ 43 \\ \hline 516 \\ +\ 6880 \\ \hline 7396 \end{array}$$ ⟶ The product of 172 and 43 is 7396.

BASIC SKILLS

Example: A student buys 4 boxes of crayons. Each box contains 16 crayons. How many total crayons does the student have?

The total number of crayons is 16 x 4.

$$\begin{array}{r} 16 \\ \times\ 4 \\ \hline 64 \end{array}$$ → Total number of crayons equals 64.

Division of whole numbers

Division, the inverse of multiplication, is another of the four basic number operations. When we divide one number by another, we determine how many times we can multiply the divisor (number divided by) before we exceed the number we are dividing (dividend). For example, 8 divided by 2 equals 4 because we can multiply 2 four times to reach 8 (2 x 4 = 8 or 2 + 2 + 2 + 2 = 8). Using the grouping conceptualization we used with multiplication, we can divide 8 into 4 groups of 2 or 2 groups of 4. We call the answer to a division problem the quotient.

If the divisor does not divide evenly into the dividend, we express the leftover amount either as a remainder or as a fraction with the divisor as the denominator. For example, 9 divided by 2 equals 4 with a remainder of 1 or 4 ½.

The basic algorithm for division is long division. We start by representing the quotient as follows.

$14\overline{)293}$ → 14 is the divisor and 293 is the dividend.

This represents 293 ÷ 14.

Next, we divide the divisor into the dividend starting from the left.

$14\overline{)293}^{\ 2}$ → 14 divides into 29 two times with a remainder.

Next, we multiply the partial quotient by the divisor, subtract this value from the first digits of the dividend, and bring down the remaining dividend digits to complete the number.

$$\begin{array}{r} 2 \\ 14\overline{)293} \\ -28 \\ \hline 13 \end{array}$$ → 2 x 14 = 28, 29 – 28 = 1, and bringing down the 3 yields 13.

Finally, we divide again (the divisor into the remaining value) and repeat the preceding process. The number left after the subtraction represents the remainder.

$$\begin{array}{r} 20 \\ 14\overline{)293} \\ -28 \\ \hline 13 \\ -0 \\ \hline 13 \end{array}$$

→ The final quotient is 20 with a remainder of 13. We can also represent this quotient as 20 13/14.

Example: Each box of apples contains 24 apples. How many boxes must a grocer purchase to supply a group of 252 people with one apple each?

The grocer needs 252 apples. Because he must buy apples in groups of 24, we divide 252 by 24 to determine how many boxes he needs to buy.

$$\begin{array}{r} 10 \\ 24\overline{)252} \\ -24 \\ \hline 12 \\ -0 \\ \hline 12 \end{array}$$

→ The quotient is 10 with a remainder of 12.

Thus, the grocer needs 10 boxes plus 12 more apples. Therefore, the minimum number of boxes the grocer can purchase is 11.

Example: At his job, John gets paid $20 for every hour he works. If John made $940 in a week, how many hours did he work?

This is a division problem. To determine the number of hours John worked, we divide the total amount made ($940) by the hourly rate of pay ($20). Thus, the number of hours worked equals 940 divided by 20.

$$\begin{array}{r} 47 \\ 20\overline{)940} \\ -80 \\ \hline 140 \\ -140 \\ \hline 0 \end{array}$$

→ 20 divides into 940, 47 times with no remainder.

John worked 47 hours.

BASIC SKILLS

Addition and Subtraction of Decimals

When adding and subtracting decimals, we align the numbers by place value as we do with whole numbers. After adding or subtracting each column, we bring the decimal down, placing it in the same location as in the numbers added or subtracted.

Example: Find the sum of 152.3 and 36.342.

$$\begin{array}{r} 152.300 \\ +36.342 \\ \hline 188.642 \end{array}$$

Note that we placed two zeroes after the final place value in 152.3 to clarify the column addition.

Example: Find the difference of 152.3 and 36.342.

$$\begin{array}{r} ^{2\ 9\ 10} \\ 152.\cancel{300} \\ -36.342 \\ \hline 58 \end{array} \longrightarrow \begin{array}{r} ^{(4)11(12)} \\ 1\cancel{5}2.\cancel{300} \\ -36.342 \\ \hline 115.958 \end{array}$$

Note how we borrowed to subtract from the zeroes in the hundredths' and thousandths' place of 152.300.

Multiplication of Decimals

When multiplying decimal numbers, we multiply exactly as with whole numbers and place the decimal moving in from the left the total number of decimal places contained in the two numbers multiplied. For example, when multiplying 1.5 and 2.35, we place the decimal in the product 3 places in from the left (3.525).

Example: Find the product of 3.52 and 4.1.

$$\begin{array}{r} 3.52 \\ \times4.1 \\ \hline 352 \\ +14080 \\ \hline 14432 \end{array}$$

→ Note that there are 3 total decimal places in the two numbers.

→ We place the decimal 3 places in from the left.

Thus, the final product is 14.432.

BASIC SKILLS

Example: A shopper has 5 one-dollar bills, 6 quarters, 3 nickels, and 4 pennies in his pocket. How much money does he have?

$$5 \times \$1.00 = \$5.00 \quad \begin{array}{c} 3 \\ \$0.25 \\ \times 6 \\ \hline \$1.50 \end{array} \quad \begin{array}{c} \$0.05 \\ \times 3 \\ \hline \$0.15 \end{array} \quad \begin{array}{c} \$0.01 \\ \times 4 \\ \hline \$0.04 \end{array}$$

Note the placement of the decimals in the multiplication products. Thus, the total amount of money in the shopper's pocket is:

$$\begin{array}{r} \$5.00 \\ 1.50 \\ 0.15 \\ +0.04 \\ \hline \$6.69 \end{array}$$

Division of Decimals

When dividing decimal numbers, we first remove the decimal in the divisor by moving the decimal in the dividend the same number of spaces to the right. For example, when dividing 1.45 into 5.3 we convert the numbers to 145 and 530 and perform normal whole number division.

Example: Find the quotient of 5.3 divided by 1.45.
Convert to 145 and 530.

Divide.

$$\begin{array}{r} 3 \\ 145\overline{)530} \\ -435 \\ \hline 95 \end{array} \longrightarrow \begin{array}{r} 3.65 \\ 145\overline{)530.00} \\ -435 \\ \hline 950 \\ -870 \\ \hline 800 \end{array}$$

Note that we insert the decimal to continue division.

Because one of the numbers divided contained one decimal place, we round the quotient to one decimal place. Thus, the final quotient is 3.7.

BASIC SKILLS

Operating with Percents

Example: 5 is what percent of 20?

This is the same as converting $\frac{5}{20}$ to % form.

$$\frac{5}{20} \times \frac{100}{1} = \frac{5}{1} \times \frac{5}{1} = 25\%$$

Example: There are 64 dogs in the kennel. 48 are collies. What percent are collies?

Restate the problem.   48 is what percent of 64?
Write an equation. $48 = n \times 64$
Solve. $\frac{48}{64} = n$

$n = \frac{3}{4} = 75\%$

75% of the dogs are collies.

Example: The auditorium was filled to 90% capacity. There were 558 seats occupied. What is the capacity of the auditorium?

Restate the problem.   90% of what number is 558?
Write an equation. $0.9n = 558$
Solve. $n = \frac{558}{.9}$
   $n = 620$

The capacity of the auditorium is 620 people.

Example: A pair of shoes costs $42.00. Sales tax is 6%. What is the total cost of the shoes?

Restate the problem.   What is 6% of 42?
Write an equation. $n = 0.06 \times 42$
Solve. $n = 2.52$

Add the sales tax to the cost. $42.00 + $2.52 = $44.52

The total cost of the shoes, including sales tax, is $44.52.

TEACHER CERTIFICATION STUDY GUIDE

Addition and subtraction of fractions

Key Points

1. You need a common denominator in order to add and subtract reduced and improper fractions.

    Example: $\dfrac{1}{3} + \dfrac{7}{3} = \dfrac{1+7}{3} = \dfrac{8}{3} = 2\dfrac{2}{3}$

    Example: $\dfrac{4}{12} + \dfrac{6}{12} - \dfrac{3}{12} = \dfrac{4+6-3}{12} = \dfrac{7}{12}$

2. Adding an integer and a fraction of the <u>same</u> sign results directly in a mixed fraction.

    Example: $2 + \dfrac{2}{3} = 2\dfrac{2}{3}$

    Example: $^-2 - \dfrac{3}{4} = ^- 2\dfrac{3}{4}$

3. Adding an integer and a fraction with different signs involves the following steps.

    - find a common denominator
    - add or subtract as needed
    - change to a mixed fraction if possible

    Example: $2 - \dfrac{1}{3} = \dfrac{2 \times 3 - 1}{3} = \dfrac{6-1}{3} = \dfrac{5}{3} = 1\dfrac{2}{3}$

Example: Add $7\dfrac{3}{8} + 5\dfrac{2}{7}$

   Add the whole numbers; add the fractions and combine the two results:

   $7\dfrac{3}{8} + 5\dfrac{2}{7} = (7+5) + (\dfrac{3}{8} + \dfrac{2}{7})$

   $= 12 + \dfrac{(7 \times 3) + (8 \times 2)}{56}$ (LCM of 8 and 7)

   $= 12 + \dfrac{21 + 16}{56} = 12 + \dfrac{37}{56} = 12\dfrac{37}{56}$

BASIC SKILLS

Example: Perform the operation.

$$\frac{2}{3} - \frac{5}{6}$$

We first find the LCM of 3 and 6 which is 6.

$$\frac{2 \times 2}{3 \times 2} - \frac{5}{6} \to \frac{4-5}{6} = \frac{-1}{6}$$

Example: $-7\frac{1}{4} + 2\frac{7}{8}$

$$-7\frac{1}{4} + 2\frac{7}{8} = (-7 + 2) + (\frac{-1}{4} + \frac{7}{8})$$

$$= (-5) + \frac{(-2+7)}{8} = (-5) + (\frac{5}{8})$$

$$= (-5) + \frac{5}{8} = \frac{-5 \times 8}{1 \times 8} + \frac{5}{8} = \frac{-40 + 5}{8}$$

$$= \frac{-35}{8} = -4\frac{3}{8}$$

Divide 35 by 8 to get 4, remainder 3.

Caution: A common error is...

$$-7\frac{1}{4} + 2\frac{7}{8} = -7\frac{2}{8} + 2\frac{7}{8} = -5\frac{9}{8} \qquad \text{Wrong.}$$

It is correct to add -7 and 2 to get -5, but adding $\frac{2}{8} + \frac{7}{8} = \frac{9}{8}$ is wrong. It should have been $\frac{-2}{8} + \frac{7}{8} = \frac{5}{8}$. Then,

$$-5 + \frac{5}{8} = -4\frac{3}{8} \text{ as before.}$$

Multiplication of fractions

Using the following example: $3\frac{1}{4} \times \frac{5}{6}$

1. Convert each number to an improper fraction.

   $3\frac{1}{4} = \frac{(12+1)}{4} = \frac{13}{4}$ $\quad\quad$ $\frac{5}{6}$ is already in reduced form.

2. Reduce (cancel) common factors of the numerator and denominator if they exist.

   $\frac{13}{4} \times \frac{5}{6}$ $\quad$ No common factors exist.

3. Multiply the numerators by each other and the denominators by each other.

   $\frac{13}{4} \times \frac{5}{6} = \frac{65}{24}$

4. If possible, reduce the fraction back to its lowest term.

   $\frac{65}{24}$ Cannot be reduced further.

5. Convert the improper fraction back to a mixed fraction by using long division.

   $\frac{65}{24} = 24\overline{)65}$ with quotient 2, 48, remainder 17 $\quad\quad = 2\frac{17}{24}$

Summary of sign changes for multiplication:

a. $(+) \times (+) = (+)$

b. $(-) \times (+) = (-)$

c. $(+) \times (-) = (-)$

d. $(-) \times (-) = (+)$

BASIC SKILLS

Example: $7\dfrac{1}{3} \times \dfrac{5}{11} = \dfrac{22}{3} \times \dfrac{5}{11}$ Reduce like terms (22 and 11)

$= \dfrac{2}{3} \times \dfrac{5}{1} = \dfrac{10}{3} = 3\dfrac{1}{3}$

Example: $^-6\dfrac{1}{4} \times \dfrac{5}{9} = \dfrac{^-25}{4} \times \dfrac{5}{9}$

$= \dfrac{^-125}{36} = ^-3\dfrac{17}{36}$

Example: $\dfrac{^-1}{4} \times \dfrac{^-3}{7}$ Negative times a negative equals a positive.

$= \dfrac{1}{4} \times \dfrac{3}{7} = \dfrac{3}{28}$

Division of fractions:

1. Change mixed fractions to improper fractions.

2. Change the division problem to a multiplication problem by using the reciprocal of the number after the division sign.

3. Find the sign of the final product.

4. Cancel common factors if they exist between the numerator and the denominator.

5. Multiply the numerators together and the denominators together.

6. Change the improper fraction to a mixed number.

Example: $3\dfrac{1}{5} \div 2\dfrac{1}{4} = \dfrac{16}{5} \div \dfrac{9}{4}$

$= \dfrac{16}{5} \times \dfrac{4}{9}$ Reciprocal of $\dfrac{9}{4}$ is $\dfrac{4}{9}$.

$= \dfrac{64}{45} = 1\dfrac{19}{45}$

BASIC SKILLS

Example: $7\dfrac{3}{4} \div 11\dfrac{5}{8} = \dfrac{31}{4} \div \dfrac{93}{8}$

$= \dfrac{31}{4} \times \dfrac{8}{93}$ Reduce like terms.

$= \dfrac{1}{1} \times \dfrac{2}{3} = \dfrac{2}{3}$

Example: $\left(-2\dfrac{1}{2}\right) \div 4\dfrac{1}{6} = \dfrac{^-5}{2} \div \dfrac{25}{6}$

$= \dfrac{^-5}{2} \times \dfrac{6}{25}$ Reduce like terms.

$= \dfrac{^-1}{1} \times \dfrac{3}{5} = \dfrac{^-3}{5}$

Example: $\left(-5\dfrac{3}{8}\right) \div \left(\dfrac{^-7}{16}\right) = \dfrac{^-43}{8} \div \dfrac{^-7}{16}$

$= \dfrac{^-43}{8} \times \dfrac{^-16}{7}$ Reduce like terms.

$= \dfrac{43}{1} \times \dfrac{2}{7}$ Negative times a negative equals a positive.

$= \dfrac{86}{7} = 12\dfrac{2}{7}$

BASIC SKILLS

Skill 1.3 **Apply basic number theory concepts including the use of primes, composites, factors, and multiples in solving problems.**

GCF is the abbreviation for the **greatest common factor**. The GCF is the largest number that is a factor of all the numbers given in a problem. The GCF can be no larger than the smallest number given in the problem. If no other number is a common factor, then the GCF will be the number 1. To find the GCF, list all possible factors of the smallest number given (include the number itself). Starting with the largest factor (which is the number itself), determine if it is also a factor of all the other given numbers. If so, that is the GCF. If that factor doesn't work, try the same method on the next smaller factor. Continue until you find a common factor. That is the GCF. Note: There can be other common factors besides the GCF.

Example: Find the GCF of 12, 20, and 36.

The smallest number in the problem is 12. The factors of 12 are 1,2,3,4,6, and 12. 12 is the largest factor, but it does not divide evenly into 20. Neither does 6, but 4 will divide into both 20 and 36 evenly.

Therefore, 4 is the GCF.

Example: Find the GCF of 14 and 15.

Factors of 14 are 1,2,7 and 14. 14 is the largest factor, but it does not divide evenly into 15. Neither does 7 or 2. Therefore, the only factor common to both 14 and 15 is the number 1, the GCF.

LCM is the abbreviation for **least common multiple**. The least common multiple of a group of numbers is the smallest number that all of the given numbers will divide into. The least common multiple will always be the largest of the given numbers or a multiple of the largest number.

Example: Find the LCM of 20, 30 and 40.

The largest number given is 40, but 30 will not divide evenly into 40. The next multiple of 40 is 80 (2 x 40), but 30 will not divide evenly into 80 either. The next multiple of 40 is 120. 120 is divisible by both 20 and 30, so 120 is the LCM (least common multiple).

Example: Find the LCM of 96, 16, and 24.

The largest number is 96. 96 is divisible by both 16 and 24, so 96 is the LCM.

BASIC SKILLS

Example: Elly Mae can feed the animals in 15 minutes. Jethro can feed them in 10 minutes. How long will it take them if they work together?

If Elly Mae can feed the animals in 15 minutes, then she could feed 1/15 of them in 1 minute, 2/15 of them in 2 minutes, $x/15$ of them in x minutes. In the same fashion Jethro could feed $x/10$ of them in x minutes. Together they complete 1 job. The equation is:

$$\frac{x}{15} + \frac{x}{10} = 1$$

Multiply each term by the LCD of 30:

$$2x + 3x = 30$$
$$x = 6 \text{ minutes}$$

Composite numbers are whole numbers that have more than 2 different factors. For example 9 is composite because besides factors of 1 and 9, 3 is also a factor. 70 is also composite because besides the factors of 1 and 70, the numbers 2,5,7,10,14, and 35 are also factors.

Prime numbers are whole numbers greater than 1 that have only 2 factors, 1 and the number itself. Examples of prime numbers are 2,3,5,7,11,13,17, or 19. Note that 2 is the only even prime number. When factoring into prime factors, all the factors must be numbers that cannot be factored again (wIthout usIng 1). Initially we can factor numbers into any 2 factors. Check each resulting factor to see if we can factor it again. Continue factoring until all remaining factors are prime. This is the list of prime factors. Regardless of what way the original number was factored, the final list of prime factors will always be the same.

Remember that the number 1 is neither prime nor composite.

Example: Factor 30 into prime factors.

Factor 30 into any 2 factors.

5 · 6   Now factor the 6.
5 · 2 · 3 These are all prime factors.

Factor 30 into any 2 factors.

3 · 10   Now factor the 10.
3 · 2 · 5 These are the same prime factors even though the original factors were different.

Example: Factor 240 into prime factors.

Factor 240 into any 2 factors.

$24 \cdot 10$ Now factor both 24 and 10.
$4 \cdot 6 \cdot 2 \cdot 5$ Now factor both 4 and 6.
$2 \cdot 2 \cdot 2 \cdot 3 \cdot 2 \cdot 5$ These are prime factors.

We can also write this as $2^4 \cdot 3 \cdot 5$.

Skill 1.4   **Apply the order of operations with or without grouping symbols.**

We must always follow **the Order of Operations** when evaluating algebraic expressions. Follow these steps in order:

1. Simplify inside grouping characters such as parentheses, brackets, square roots, fraction bars, etc.

2. Multiply out expressions with exponents.

3. Do multiplication or division, from left to right.

4. Do addition or subtraction, from left to right.

Example: $3^3 - 5(b+2)$

$= 3^3 - 5b - 10$

$= 27 - 5b - 10 = 17 - 5b$

Example: $2 - 4 \times 2^3 - 2(4 - 2 \times 3)$

$= 2 - 4 \times 2^3 - 2(4-6) = 2 - 4 \times 2^3 - 2(^-2)$

$= 2 - 4 \times 2^3 + 4 = 2 - 4 \times 8 + 4$

$= 2 - 32 + 4 = 6 - 32 = ^-26$

TEACHER CERTIFICATION STUDY GUIDE

COMPETENCY 2.0 KNOWLEDGE OF MEASUREMENT (USING CUSTOMARY OR METRIC UNITS)

Skill 2.1 Solve real-world problems involving length, weight, mass, perimeter, area, capacity, and volume.

Measurements of length (English system)

12 inches (in)	=	1 foot (ft)
3 feet (ft)	=	1 yard (yd)
1760 yards (yd)	=	1 mile (mi)

Measurements of length (Metric system)

1 kilometer (km)	=	1000 meters (m)
1 hectometer (hm)	=	100 meters (m)
1 decameter (dam)	=	10 meters (m)
1 meter (m)	=	1 meter (m)
1 decimeter (dm)	=	1/10 meter (m)
1 centimeter (cm)	=	1/100 meter (m)
1 millimeter (mm)	=	1/1000 meter (m)

Conversion of length from English to Metric

1 inch	=	2.54 centimeters
1 foot	≈	30 centimeters
1 yard	≈	0.9 meters
1 mile	≈	1.6 kilometers

Measurements of weight (English system)

28 grams (g)	=	1 ounce (oz)
16 ounces (oz)	=	1 pound (lb)
2000 pounds (lb)	=	1 ton (t)

Measurements of weight (Metric system)

1 kilogram (kg)	=	1000 grams (g)
1 gram (g)	=	1 gram (g)
1 milligram (mg)	=	1/1000 gram (g)

Conversion of weight from English to Metric

1 ounce	≈	28 grams
1 pound	≈	0.45 kilograms
	≈	454 grams

Measurement of volume (English system)

8 fluid ounces (oz)	=	1 cup (c)
2 cups (c)	=	1 pint (pt)
2 pints (pt)	=	1 quart (qt)
4 quarts (qt)	=	1 gallon (gal)

Measurement of volume (Metric system)

1 kiloliter (kl)	=	1000 liters (l)
1 liter (l)	=	1 liter (l)
1 milliliter (ml)	=	1/1000 liters (ml)

Conversion of volume from English to Metric

1 teaspoon (tsp)	≈	5 milliliters
1 fluid ounce	≈	15 milliliters
1 cup	≈	0.24 liters
1 pint	≈	0.47 liters
1 quart	≈	0.95 liters
1 gallon	≈	3.8 liters

Measurement of time

1 minute	=	60 seconds
1 hour	=	60 minutes
1 day	=	24 hours
1 week	=	7 days
1 year	=	365 days
1 century	=	100 years

Note: (') represents feet and (") represents inches.

BASIC SKILLS

We can derive **square units** with knowledge of basic units of length by squaring the equivalent measurements.

> 1 square foot (sq. ft.) = 144 sq. in.
> 1 sq. yd. = 9 sq. ft.
> 1 sq. yd. = 1296 sq. in.

Example:

14 sq. yd. = _____ sq. ft.
14 × 9 = 126 sq. ft.

Weight

Example: Kathy has a bag of potatoes that weighs 5 lbs., 10 oz. She uses one third of the bag to make mashed potatoes. How much does the bag weigh now?

1 lb. = 16 oz.
5(16 oz.) + 10 oz.
= 80 oz + 10 oz = 90 oz. (starting weight of bag)
$90 - (\frac{1}{3})90$ oz.
= 90 oz. − 30 oz.
= 60 oz.
60 ÷ 16 = 3.75 lbs.

Polygons

The **perimeter** of any polygon is the sum of the lengths of the sides.

The **area** of a polygon is the number of square units covered by the figure.

FIGURE	AREA FORMULA	PERIMETER FORMULA
Rectangle	Length x Width	2(Length + Width)
Triangle	$\frac{1}{2}bh$ (b = base, h = height)	$a+b+c$ (where a, b, and c are legs of the triangle)
Parallelogram	bh	sum of the lengths of the sides
Trapezoid	$\frac{1}{2}h(a+b)$ (where a and b are the bases)	sum of the lengths of the sides

BASIC SKILLS

Perimeter of a Polygon

Example: A farmer has a piece of land shaped as shown below. He wishes to fence this land. The estimated cost is $25 per linear foot. What is the total cost of fencing this property to the nearest foot.

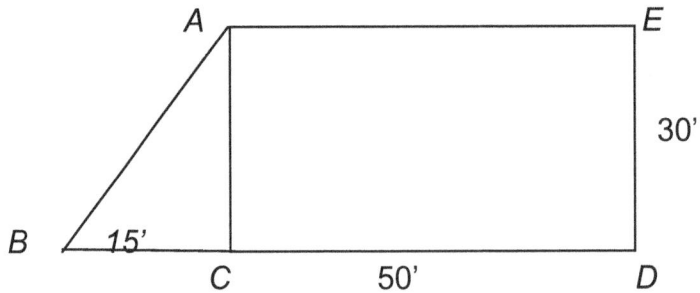

From the right triangle ABC, AC = 30 and BC = 15.

Since $(AB)^2 = (AC)^2 + (BC)^2$
$(AB)^2 = (30)^2 + (15)^2$

So, $\sqrt{(AB)^2} = AB = \sqrt{30^2 + 15^2} = \sqrt{1125} = 33.5410$ feet

To the nearest foot AB = 34 feet.

Perimeter of the piece of land is $= AB + BC + CD + DE + EA$

= 34 + 15 + 50 + 30 + 50 = 179 feet

cost of fencing = $25 x 179 = $4,475.00

Area of a Polygon

Example: What is the cost of carpeting a rectangular office that measures 12 feet by 15 feet if the carpet costs $12.50 per square yard?

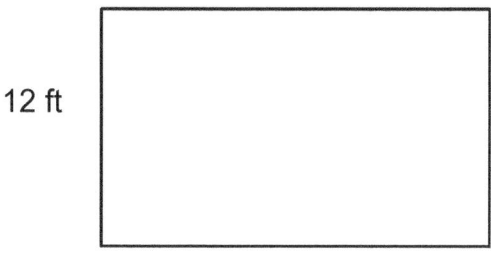

12 ft

15 ft

This is a basic area problem. To solve this problem you must first determine the area of the office. The area of a rectangle is the *length* times the *width*.

Substitute the given values in the equation $A = lw$

$$A = (12 \text{ ft})(15 \text{ ft})$$

$$A = 180 \text{ ft}^2$$

The problem asked you to determine the cost of carpet at $12.50 per square yard.

First, you need to convert 180 ft.^{2} into yards^2.

1 yd. = 3 ft.

(1 yard)(1 yard) = (3 feet)(3 feet)

1 yd^2 = 9 ft^2

Hence, 180 ft^2 = 20 yd^2 (180 ÷ 9)

The carpet cost $12.50 per square yard; thus, the cost of carpeting the office is $12.50 × 20 yd^2 = $250.00.

Example: Find the area of a parallelogram with bases 6.5 cm long and altitude 3.7 cm long. (note: the altitude is the line perpendicular to the bases)

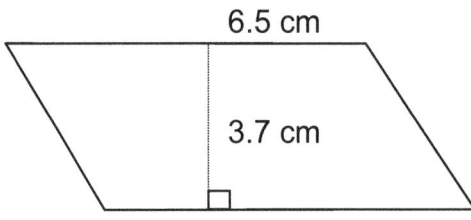

$A_{parallelogram}$ = bh
= (3.7)(6.5)
= 24.05 cm^2

Example: Find the area of this triangle.

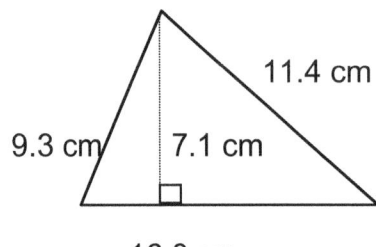

$A_{triangle} = \frac{1}{2}bh$
= 0.5 (16.8) (7.1)
= 59.64 cm^2

Example: Find the area of this trapezoid.

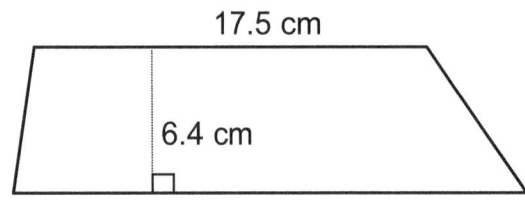

The area of a trapezoid equals one-half the sum of the bases times the altitude.

$A_{trapezoid} = \frac{1}{2}h(b_1 + b_2)$
= 0.5 (6.4) (17.5 + 23.7)
= 131.84 cm^2

BASIC SKILLS

Circles

The distance around a circle is the **circumference**. The ratio of the circumference to the diameter is represented by the Greek letter pi (π).

$$\pi \approx 3.14 \approx \frac{22}{7}$$

The formula used to find the circumference of a circle is $C = 2\pi r$ or $C = \pi d$ where r is the radius of the circle and d is the diameter.

The formula used to find the **area** of a circle is $A = \pi r^2$.

Example: Find the circumference and area of a circle whose radius is 7 meters.

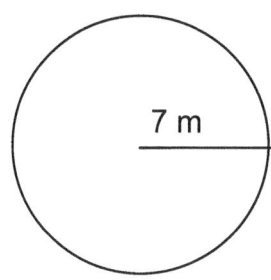

$C = 2\pi r$
$= 2(3.14)(7)$
$= 43.96$ m

$A = \pi r^2$
$= 3.14(7)(7)$
$= 153.86$ m^2

The following are formulas used to compute **Volume** and **Surface area**:

FIGURE	VOLUME	TOTAL SURFACE AREA
Right Cylinder	$\pi r^2 h$	$2\pi rh + 2\pi r^2$
Right Cone	$\dfrac{\pi r^2 h}{3}$	$\pi r \sqrt{r^2 + h^2} + \pi r^2$
Sphere	$\dfrac{4}{3}\pi r^3$	$4\pi r^2$
Rectangular Solid	LWH	$2LW + 2WH + 2LH$

BASIC SKILLS

TEACHER CERTIFICATION STUDY GUIDE

FIGURE	LATERAL AREA	TOTAL AREA	VOLUME
Regular Pyramid	1/2Pl	1/2Pl+B	1/3Bh

P = Perimeter
h = height
B = Area of Base
l = slant height

Example: What is the volume of a shoe box with a length of 35 cm, a width of 20 cm and a height of 15 cm?

Volume of a rectangular solid
= Length x Width x Height
= 35 x 20 x 15
= 10500 cm^3

Example: A water company is trying to decide whether to use traditional cylindrical paper cups or to offer conical paper cups since both cost the same amount. The traditional cups are 8 cm wide and 14 cm high. The conical cups are 12 cm wide and 19 cm high. The company will use the cup that holds the most water.

Draw and label a sketch of each.

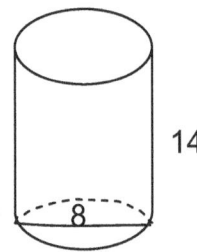
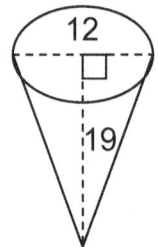

$V = \pi r^2 h$ $V = \dfrac{\pi r^2 h}{3}$ 1. write formula

$V = \pi(4)^2(14)$ $V = \dfrac{1}{3}\pi(6)^2(19)$ 2. substitute

$V = 703.717$ cm^3 $V = 716.283$ cm^3 3. solve

The choice should be the conical cup, because it has a greater volume and can hold more water.

BASIC SKILLS   28

Example: How much material is needed to make a basketball that has a diameter of 15 inches? How much air is needed to fill the basketball?

Draw and label a sketch.

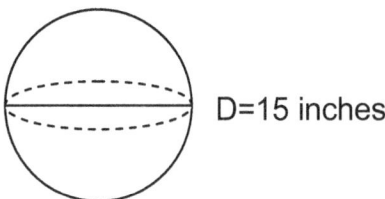 D=15 inches

The amount of material needed is equal to the surface area and the amount of air needed is equal to the volume.

Total surface area   Volume

$TSA = 4\pi r^2$ $V = \dfrac{4}{3}\pi r^3$ 1. write formula

$= 4\pi(7.5)^2$ $= \dfrac{4}{3}\pi(7.5)^3$ 2. substitute

$= 706.8 \text{ in}^2$ $= 1767.1 \text{ in}^3$ 3. solve

Skill 2.2 **Solve real-world problems involving rated measures (e.g., miles per hour, meters per second, cost per item, and cost per unit).**

Example: A class wants to take a field trip from New York City to Albany. The trip is approximately 160 miles. If they travel at 50 miles per hour, how long will it take for them to get there (assuming traveling at a steady rate)?

Set up the equation as a proportion and solve:

$\dfrac{160 \text{ miles}}{x \text{ hours}} = \dfrac{50 \text{ miles}}{1 \text{ hour}}$

(160 miles)(1 hour) = (50 miles) (*x* hours)

160 = 50*x*

x = 3.2 hours

Example: A salesman drove 480 miles from Pittsburgh to Hartford. The next day he returned the same distance to Pittsburgh in half an hour less time than his original trip took, because he increased his average speed by 4 mph. Find his original speed.

Since distance = (rate)(time) then time = $\dfrac{\text{distance}}{\text{rate}}$

original time $-$ 1/2 hour = shorter return time

$$\dfrac{480}{x} - \dfrac{1}{2} = \dfrac{480}{x+4}$$

Multiplying by the LCD of $2x(x+4)$, the equation becomes:
$480\big[2(x+4)\big] - 1\big[x(x+4)\big] = 480(2x)$
$960x + 3840 - x^2 - 4x = 960x$
$x^2 + 4x - 3840 = 0$
$(x+64)(x-60) = 0$
$x = 60$ 60 mph is the original speed
         64 mph is the faster return speed

Cost per unit

The unit rate for purchasing an item is its price divided by the number of pounds/ounces, etc. in the item. The item with the lower unit rate is the lower price. See Skill 3.2 for further information.

Example: Find the item with the best unit price:

$1.79 for 10 ounces
$1.89 for 12 ounces
$5.49 for 32 ounces

$\dfrac{1.79}{10} = .179$ per ounce $\dfrac{1.89}{12} = .1575$ per ounce $\dfrac{5.49}{32} = .172$ per ounce

$1.89 for 12 ounces is the best price.

BASIC SKILLS

TEACHER CERTIFICATION STUDY GUIDE

Skill 2.3   **Solve real-world problems involving scaled drawings (e.g., maps, blueprints, and models).**

Students need to understand the use of ratios and proportions to create scale models of real-life objects, the principles of ratio and proportion, and how to calculate scale using ratio and proportion.

Scaled drawings (maps, blueprints, and models) have many real-world applications. Architects make blueprints and models of buildings. Contractors then use these drawings and models to build the buildings. Engineers make scaled drawings of bridges, machine parts, roads, and airplanes. Maps of the world, countries, states, and roads are scaled drawings. Landscape designers use scaled drawings and models of plants, decks, and other structures to show how they should be placed around a house or other building. Models of cars, boats, and planes made from kits are scaled. Automobile engineers construct models of cars before the actual assembly. Many museum exhibits are actually scaled models because the real size of the items would be too large.

Examples of real-world problems that students might solve using scaled drawings include:

- reading road maps and determining the distance between locations by using the map scale,
- creating a scaled drawing (floor plan) of their classroom to determine the best use of space,
- creating an 8 ½" x 11" representation of a quilt
- drawing a blueprint of their rooms and creating a model from it

Skill 2.4   **Solve real-world problems involving the change of units of measures of length, weight, capacity, and time.**

Length

Example: A car skidded 170 yards on an icy road before coming to a stop. How long is the skid distance in kilometers?

Since 1 yard $\approx$ 0.9 meters, multiply 170 yards by 0.9.

$$170 \times 0.9 = 153 \text{ meters}$$

Since 1000 meters = 1 kilometer, divide 153 by 1000.

$$\frac{153}{1000} = 0.153 \text{ kilometers}$$

BASIC SKILLS

Example: The distance around a race course is exactly 1 mile, 17 feet, and $9\frac{1}{4}$ inches. Approximate this distance to the nearest tenth of a foot.

Convert the distance to feet.

$$1 \text{ mile} = 1760 \text{ yards} = 1760 \times 3 \text{ feet} = 5280 \text{ feet.}$$

$$9\frac{1}{4} \text{ inches} = \frac{37}{4} \times \frac{1}{12} = \frac{37}{48} \approx 0.77083 \text{ feet}$$

So 1 mile, 17 feet and $9\frac{1}{4}$ inches $= 5280 + 17 + 0.77083$ feet

$$= 5297.\underline{7}7083 \text{ feet.}$$

Now, we need to round to the nearest tenth digit. The underlined 7 is in the tenth place. The digit in the hundredth place, also a 7, is greater than 5. Thus, we should round the 7 in the tenths place needs to up to 8 to get a final answer of 5297.8 feet.

Weight

Example: Zachary weighs 150 pounds. Tom weighs 153 pounds. What is the difference in their weights in grams?

153 pounds – 150 pounds = 3 pounds
1 pound = 454 grams
3(454 grams) = 1362 grams

Capacity

Example: Students in a fourth grade class want to fill a 3 gallon jug using cups of water. How many cups of water will they need?

1 gallon = 16 cups of water
3 gallons x 16 cups = 48 cups of water

Time

Example: It takes Cynthia 45 minutes to get ready each morning. How many hours does she spend getting ready each week?

45 minutes X 7 days = 315 minutes

$$\frac{315 \text{ minutes}}{60 \text{ minutes in an hour}} = 5.25 \text{ hours}$$

BASIC SKILLS

TEACHER CERTIFICATION STUDY GUIDE

Skill 2.5   Solve real-world problems involving estimates of measures including length, weight, mass, temperature, time, money, perimeter, area, and volume.

To estimate measurement of familiar objects, it is first necessary to determine the units to use.

Examples:
Length
1. The coastline of Florida
2. The width of a ribbon
3. The thickness of a book
4. The depth of water in a pool

Weight or mass
1. A bag of sugar
2. A school bus
3. A dime

Capacity or volume
1. Paint in a paint can
2. Glass of milk

Money
1. Cost of a house
2. Cost of a cup of coffee
3. Exchange rate

Perimeter
1. The edge of a backyard
2. The edge of a football field

Area
1. The size of a carpet
2. The size of a state

Example: Estimate the measurements of the following objects:

Length of a dollar bill	6 inches
Weight of a baseball	1 pound
Distance from New York to Florida	1100 km
Volume of water to fill a medicine dropper	1 milliliter
Length of a desk	2 meters
Temperature of water in a swimming pool	80° F

BASIC SKILLS   33

Depending on the degree of accuracy needed, we can measure an object with different units. For example, a pencil may be 6 inches to the nearest inch or 6 3/8 inches to the nearest eighth of an inch. Similarly, it might be 15 cm to the nearest cm or 154 mm to the nearest mm.

Given a set of objects and their measurements, the use of rounding procedures is helpful when attempting to round to the nearest given unit. When rounding to a given place value, it is necessary to look at the number in the next smaller place. If this number is 5 or more, we increase the number in the place we are rounding and change all numbers to the right to zero. If the number is less than 5, the we leave the number in the place we are rounding the same and change all numbers to the right to zero.

One method of rounding measurements can require an additional step. First, we must convert the measurement to a decimal number. Then, we apply the rules for rounding.

Example: Round the measurements to the given units.

MEASUREMENT	ROUND TO NEAREST	ANSWER
1 foot 7 inches	foot	2 ft
5 pound 6 ounces	pound	5 pounds
5 9/16 inches	inch	6 inches

Convert each measurement to a decimal number, then apply the rules for rounding.

1 foot 7 inches = $1\frac{7}{12}$ ft = 1.58333 ft, round up to 2 ft

5 pounds 6 ounces = $5\frac{6}{16}$ pounds = 5.375 pound, round to 5 pounds

$5\frac{9}{16}$ inches = 5.5625 inches, round up to 6 inches

Rounding numbers is a form of estimation that is very useful in many mathematical operations. For example, when estimating the sum of two three-digit numbers, it is helpful to round the two numbers to the nearest hundred prior to addition. We can round numbers to any place value.

Rounding whole numbers

To round whole numbers, you first find the place value you want to round to (the rounding digit) and look at the digit directly to the right. If the digit is less than five, do not change the rounding digit and replace all numbers after the rounding digit with zeroes. If the digit is greater than or equal to five, increase the rounding digit by one and replace all numbers after the rounding digit with zeroes.

Example: Round 517 to the nearest ten.

1 is the rounding digit because it occupies the tens' place.

517 rounded to the nearest ten = 520; because 7 > 5 we add one to the rounding digit.

Example: Round 15,449 to the nearest hundred.

The first 4 is the rounding digit because it occupies the hundreds' place.

15,449 rounded to the nearest hundred = 15,400, because 4 < 5 we do not add to the rounding digit.

Rounding decimals

Rounding decimals is identical to rounding whole numbers except that you simply drop all the digits to the right of the rounding digit.

Example: Round 417.3621 to the nearest tenth.

3 is the rounding digit because it occupies the tenth place.

417.3621 rounded to the nearest tenth = 417.4; because 6 > 5 we add one to the rounding digit.

Regrouping to Estimate Differences

We can estimate the difference of two numbers by first rounding the numbers and then subtracting the rounded numbers. When subtracting two rounded numbers, one rounded up and the other rounded down, we can improve our estimate by regrouping. For example, when estimating the difference of 540 and 355, we round 540 down to 500 and 355 up to 400. Thus, our estimated difference is 500 minus 400, or 100. Note that we rounded 540 down by 40 and 355 up by 45. Thus, the total amount of rounding is 85. Rounding 85 up to 100 and adding this rounded sum to 100 (our original estimate) gives us a final estimated difference of 200. This is closer to the actual difference of 185 (540 – 355). The regrouping method of estimation only works when we round the two numbers in opposite directions.

Front End Estimation

While we can add or subtract rounded numbers to estimate sums and differences, another method, front-end estimation, is simpler and usually delivers results that are just as accurate. Front-end estimation is an elementary form of estimation of sums and differences. To estimate a sum or difference by front-end estimation, we add or subtract only the two highest place values and filling the remaining place values with zeroes.

Example: Estimate 4987 + 3512 by front-end estimation.

The estimated sum is 8400 (4900 + 3500).

Note that we do not round the numbers, but merely drop the digits after the two highest place values. In other words, we convert 4987 to 4900, not 5000.

Example: Estimate 3894 – 617 by front-end estimation.

The estimated difference is 3200 (3800 – 600).

Note that because 617 does not have a digit in the thousands place and 3894 does, we convert 617 to 600, not 610.

Applied Estimation Example

Janet goes into a store to purchase a CD on sale for $13.95. While shopping, she sees two pairs of shoes, prices $19.95 and $14.50. She only has $50. Can she purchase everything?

Solve by rounding:

$19.95 → $20.00
$14.50 → $15.00
$13.95 → $14.00
$49.00   Yes, she can purchase the CD and the shoes.

Skill 2.6 **Choose the correct reading, to a specified degree of accuracy, using instruments (e.g., scales, rulers, thermometers, measuring cups, protractors, and gauges).**

When reading an instrument, students should first determine the interval of scale on the instrument. To achieve the greatest accuracy, they should read the scale to the nearest measurement mark.

If you are using a scale with a needle that has a mirrored plate behind it, view the scale so that the needle's reflection is hidden behind the needle itself. Do not look at it from an angle. In order to read a balance scale accurately, place the scale on a level surface and make sure that the hand points precisely at 0. Place objects on the plate gently and take them away gently. Face the dial straight on to read the graduation accurately. Students should read from the large graduation to smaller graduation. If the dial hand points between two graduations, they should choose the number that is closest to the hand.

When reading inches on a ruler, the student needs to understand that each inch is divided into halves by the longest mark in the middle, into fourths by the next longest marks, into eighths by the next, and into sixteenths by the shortest. When the measurement falls between two inch marks, they can give the whole number of inches, count the additional fractional marks, and give the answer as the number and fraction of inches. Remind students that the convention is always to express a fraction by its lowest possible denominator.

If students are using the metric system on a ruler, have them focus on the marks between the whole numbers (centimeters). Point out that each centimeter is broken into tenths, with the mark in the middle being longer to indicate a halfway mark. Students should learn to measure things accurately to the nearest tenth of a centimeter, then the nearest hundredth, and finally the nearest thousandth. Measurements using the metric system should always be written using the decimal system, e.g., 3.756 centimeters.

When reading a thermometer, hold it vertically at eye level. Students should check the scale of the thermometer to make certain they read as many significant digits as possible. Thermometers with heavy or extended lines that are marked 10, 20, 30, etc. should be read to the nearest 0.1 degree. Thermometers with fine lines every two degrees may be read to the nearest 0.5 degree.

In order to get an accurate reading in a liquid measuring cup, set the cup on a level surface and read it at eye level. Read the measurement at the bottom of the concave arc at the liquid's surface (the meniscus line). When measuring dry ingredients, dip the appropriate size measuring cup into the ingredient and sweep away the excess across the top with a straight-edged object.

Protractors measure angles in degrees. To measure accurately, find the center hole on the straight edge of the protractor and place it over the vertex of the angle you wish to measure. Line up the zero on the straight edge with one of the sides of the angle. Find the point where the second side of the angle intersects the curved edge of the protractor and read the number that is written at the point of intersection.

When reading an instrument such as a rain gauge, it is again important to read at eye level and at the base of the meniscus. The measuring tube is divided, marked, and labeled in tenths and hundredths. The greatest number of decimal places you will have is two.

COMPETENCY 3.0 KNOWLEDGE OF GEOMETRY AND SPATIAL SENSE

Skill 3.1 Identify and/or classify simple two-and three-dimensional figures according to their properties.

Polygons are simple closed **two-dimensional figures** composed of line segments. Their names correlate to the number of sides they have.

A **quadrilateral** is a polygon with four sides.
The sum of the measures of the angles of a quadrilateral is 360°.

A **trapezoid** is a quadrilateral with exactly <u>one</u> pair of parallel sides.

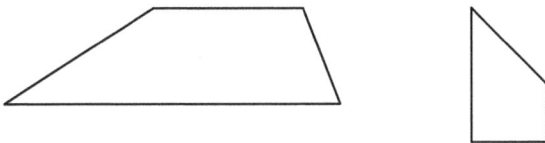

In an **isosceles trapezoid**, the non-parallel sides are congruent.

A **parallelogram** is a quadrilateral with <u>two</u> pairs of parallel sides.

In a parallelogram:
The diagonals bisect each other.
Each diagonal divides the parallelogram into two congruent triangles.
Both pairs of opposite sides are congruent.
Both pairs of opposite angles are congruent.
Two adjacent angles are supplementary.

A **rectangle** is a parallelogram with a right angle.

A **rhombus** is a parallelogram with all sides of equal length.

A **square** is a rectangle with all sides of equal length.

Example: True or false?

All squares are rhombuses.	True
All parallelograms are rectangles.	False - <u>some</u> parallelograms are rectangles
All rectangles are parallelograms.	True
Some rhombuses are squares.	True
Some rectangles are trapezoids.	False - only <u>one</u> pair of parallel sides
All quadrilaterals are parallelograms.	False - some quadrilaterals are parallelograms
Some squares are rectangles.	False - all squares are rectangles
Some parallelograms are rhombuses.	True

A **triangle** is a polygon with three sides.

We can classify triangles by the types of angles or the lengths of their sides.

An **acute** triangle has exactly three *acute* angles.
A **right** triangle has one *right* angle.
An **obtuse** triangle has one *obtuse* angle.

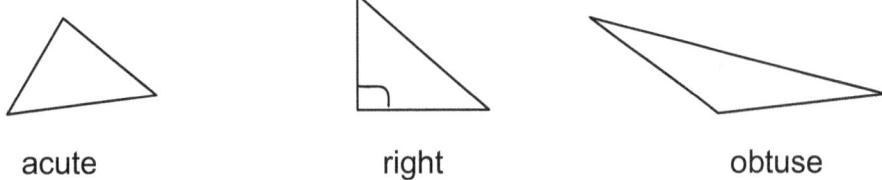

acute   right   obtuse

All *three* sides of an **equilateral** triangle are the same length.
Two sides of an **isosceles** triangle are the same length.
None of the sides of a **scalene** triangle are the same length.

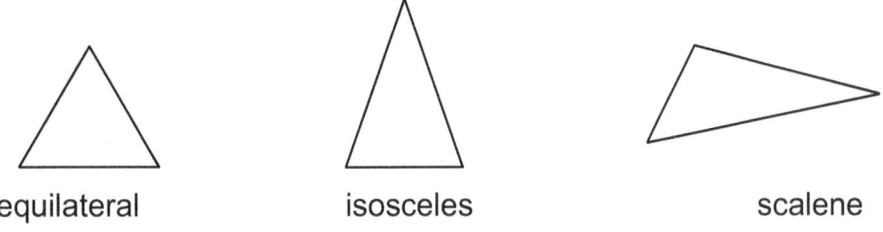

equilateral   isosceles   scalene

Example: Can a triangle have two right angles?
No. A right angle measures 90°, therefore the sum of two right angles would be 180° and there could not be third angle.

Example: Can a triangle have two obtuse angles?
No. Since an obtuse angle measures more than 90° the sum of two obtuse angles would be greater than 180°.

A **cylinder** has two congruent circular bases that are parallel.

A **sphere** is a three-dimensional figure having all its points the same distance from the center.

A **cone** is a three-dimensional figure having a circular base and a single vertex.

A **pyramid** is a three-dimensional figure with a square base and 4 triangle-shaped sides.

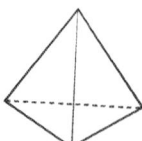

A **tetrahedron** is a 4-sided three-dimensional triangle. Each face is a triangle.

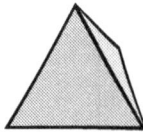

A **prism** is a three-dimensional figure with two congruent, parallel bases that are polygons.

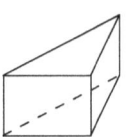

TEACHER CERTIFICATION STUDY GUIDE

Skill 3.2   Solve real-world and mathematical problems involving ratio, proportion, similarity, congruence, and the Pythagorean relationship.

A **ratio** is a comparison of 2 numbers. If a class had 11 boys and 14 girls, we can write the ratio of boys to girls in 3 ways:

$$11:14 \quad \text{or} \quad 11 \text{ to } 14 \quad \text{or} \quad \frac{11}{14}$$

The ratio of girls to boys is:

$$14:11, \; 14 \text{ to } 11 \text{ or } \; \frac{14}{11}$$

We should reduce ratios when possible. A ratio of 12 cats to 18 dogs reduces to 2:3, 2 to 3, or $2/3$.

Note: Read ratio questions carefully. Given a group of 6 adults and 5 children, the ratio of children to the entire group would be 5:11.

A **proportion** is an equation in which one fraction is set equal to another. To solve the proportion, multiply each numerator by the other fraction's denominator. Set these two products equal to each other and solve the resulting equation. This is called **cross-multiplying** the proportion.

Example: $\dfrac{4}{15} = \dfrac{x}{60}$ is a proportion.

        To solve, cross multiply.

        $(4)(60) = (15)(x)$

        $240 = 15x$

        $16 = x$

Example: $\dfrac{x+3}{3x+4} = \dfrac{2}{5}$ is a proportion.

        To solve, cross multiply.

        $5(x+3) = 2(3x+4)$

        $5x + 15 = 6x + 8$

        $7 = x$

BASIC SKILLS

Example: $\dfrac{x+2}{8} = \dfrac{2}{x-4}$ is another proportion.

To solve, cross multiply.

$(x+2)(x-4) = 8(2)$
$x^2 - 2x - 8 = 16$
$x^2 - 2x - 24 = 0$
$(x-6)(x+4) = 0$
$x = 6$ or $x = {}^-4$

We can use **proportions** to solve word problems that involve comparisons of relationships. Some situations include scale drawings and maps, similar polygons, speed, time and distance, cost, and comparison shopping.

Example: Which is the better buy, 6 items for $1.29 or 8 items for $1.69?

Find the unit price.

$\dfrac{6}{1.29} = \dfrac{1}{x}$ $\qquad$ $\dfrac{8}{1.69} = \dfrac{1}{x}$
$6x = 1.29$ $\qquad\qquad$ $8x = 1.69$
$x = 0.215$ $\qquad\qquad$ $x = 0.21125$

Thus, 8 items for $1.69 is the better buy (lower unit price).

Example: A car travels 125 miles in 2.5 hours. How far will it go in 6 hours?

Write a proportion comparing the distance and time.

$\dfrac{miles}{hours} \qquad \dfrac{125}{2.5} = \dfrac{x}{6}$

$2.5x = 750$
$x = 300$

Thus, the car can travel 300 miles in 6 hours.

Example: The scale on a map is ¾ inch = 6 miles. What is the actual distance between two cities if they are 1 ½ inches apart on the map?

Write a proportion comparing the scale to the actual distance.

$$\begin{array}{cc} \text{scale} & \text{actual} \end{array}$$

$$\frac{\frac{3}{4}}{1\frac{1}{2}} = \frac{6}{x}$$

$$\frac{3}{4}x = 1\frac{1}{2} \times 6$$

$$\frac{3}{4}x = 9$$

$$x = 12$$

Thus, the actual distance between the cities is 12 miles.

Congruent figures have the same size and shape. Congruent lines have the same length. Congruent angles have equal measures.
The symbol for congruent is ≅.

Polygons (pentagons) *ABCDE* and *VWXYZ* are congruent. They are exactly the same size and shape.

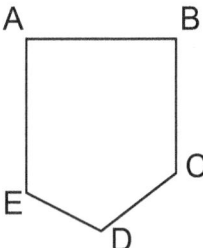
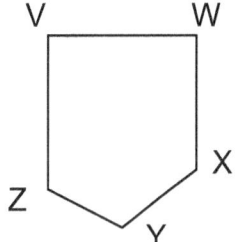

ABCDE ≅ *VWXYZ*

Corresponding parts are those congruent angles and congruent sides, that is:

corresponding angles	corresponding sides
∠A ↔ ∠V	AB ↔ VW
∠B ↔ ∠W	BC ↔ WX
∠C ↔ ∠X	CD ↔ XY
∠D ↔ ∠Y	DE ↔ YZ
∠E ↔ ∠Z	AE ↔ VZ

Similarity

Two figures that have the same shape are **similar**. Polygons are similar if and only if corresponding angles are congruent and corresponding sides are in proportion. Corresponding parts of similar polygons are proportional.

Example: Given the rectangles below, compare the area and perimeter.

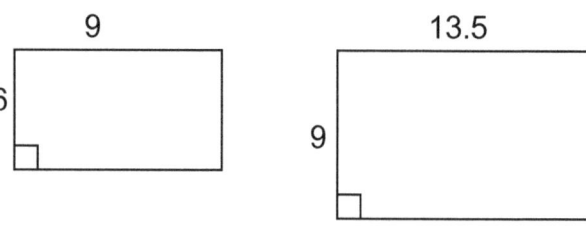

$A = LW$	$A = LW$	1. write formula
$A = (6)(9)$	$A = (9)(13.5)$	2. substitute known values
$A = 54$ sq. units	$A = 121.5$ sq. units	3. compute
$P = 2(L + W)$	$P = 2(L + W)$	1. write formula
$P = 2(6 + 9)$	$P = 2(9 + 13.5)$	2. substitute known values
$P = 30$ units	$P = 45$ units	3. compute

Notice that the areas relate to each other in the following manner:

Ratio of sides $9/13.5 = 2/3$

Multiply the first area by the square of the reciprocal $(3/2)^2$ to get the second area.

$$54 \times (3/2)^2 = 121.5$$

The perimeters relate to each other in the following manner:

Ratio of sides $9/13.5 = 2/3$

Multiply the perimeter of the first by the reciprocal of the ratio to get the perimeter of the second.

$$30 \times 3/2 = 45$$

Example: Given two similar quadrilaterals. Find the lengths of sides x, y, and z.

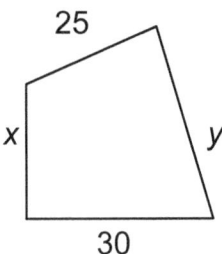 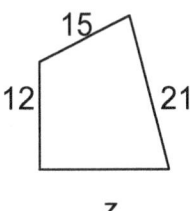

Since corresponding sides are proportional:

$$\frac{12}{x} = \frac{3}{5} \qquad \frac{21}{y} = \frac{3}{5} \qquad \frac{z}{30} = \frac{3}{5}$$

$$3x = 60 \qquad 3y = 105 \qquad 5z = 90$$
$$x = 20 \qquad y = 35 \qquad z = 18$$

Example: Tommy draws and cuts out 2 triangles for a school project. One of them has sides of 3, 6, and 9 inches. The other triangle has sides of 2, 4, and 6. Is there a relationship between the two triangles?

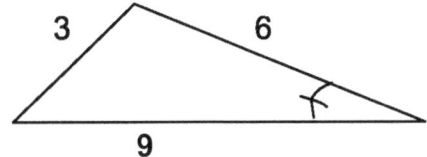 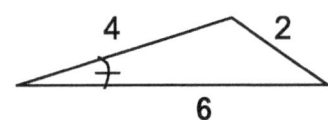

Take the proportion of the corresponding sides.

$$\frac{2}{3} \qquad \frac{4}{6} = \frac{2}{3} \qquad \frac{6}{9} = \frac{2}{3}$$

The smaller triangle is 2/3 the size of the large triangle.

The Pythagorean Theorem

Given any right triangle, $\triangle ABC$, the square of the hypotenuse is equal to the sum of the squares of the other two sides.

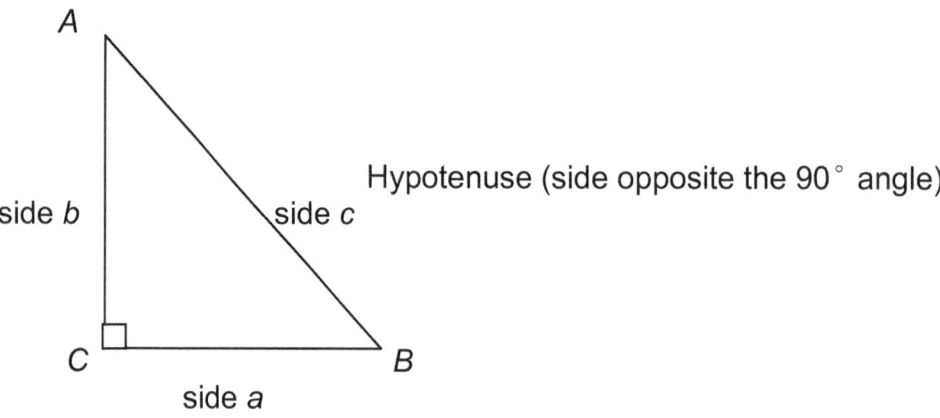

Hypotenuse (side opposite the 90° angle)

This theorem says that $(AB)^2 = (BC)^2 + (AC)^2$

or

$c^2 = a^2 + b^2$

Example: Find the area and perimeter of a rectangle if its length is 12 inches and its diagonal is 15 inches.

1. Draw and label sketch.

2. Since still need to find the height, use Pythagorean formula find the missing leg of the triangle.

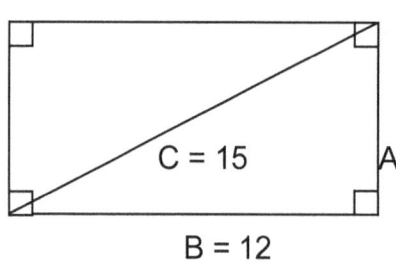

C = 15
B = 12

$A^2 + B^2 = C^2$
$A^2 + 12^2 = 15^2$
$A^2 = 15^2 - 12^2$
$A^2 = 81$
$A = 9$

Now use this information to find the area and perimeter.

$A = LW$	$P = 2(L+W)$	1. write formula
$A = (12)(9)$	$P = 2(12+9)$	2. substitute
$A = 108 \text{ in}^2$	$P = 42$ inches	3. solve

BASIC SKILLS

Example: Two old cars leave a road intersection at the same time. One car traveled due north at 55 mph while the other car traveled due east. After 3 hours, the cars were 180 miles apart. Find the speed of the second car.

Using a right triangle to represent the problem we get the figure:

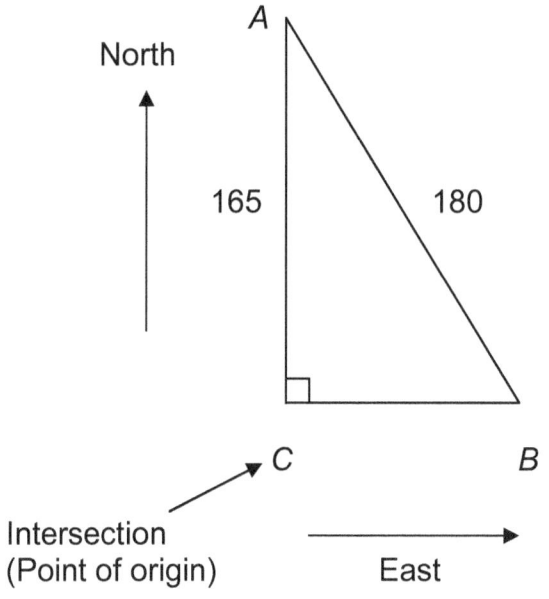

Traveling at 55 mph for 3 hours, the northbound car has driven (55)(3)=165 miles. This is the side AC.

The cars are 180 miles apart. This is side AB.

Since △ABC is a right triangle, then, by Pythagorean Theorem, we get:

$$(AB)^2 = (BC)^2 + (AC)^2 \text{ or}$$
$$(BC)^2 = (AB)^2 - (AC)^2$$

$$(BC)^2 = 180^2 - 165^2$$
$$(BC)^2 = 32400 - 27225$$
$$(BC)^2 = 5175$$

Take the square root of both sides to get:

$$\sqrt{(BC)^2} = \sqrt{5175} \approx 71.935 \text{ miles}$$

Since the east bound car has traveled 71.935 miles in 3 hours, then the average speed is:

$$\frac{71.935}{3} \approx 23.97 \text{ mph}$$

Skill 3.3 Identify the location of ordered pairs of integers in all four quadrants of a coordinate system (graph) and use the coordinate system to apply the concepts of slope and distance to solve problems.

Coordinate plane - A plane with a point selected as an origin, some length selected as a unit of distance, and two perpendicular lines that intersect at the origin, with positive and negative direction selected on each line. Traditionally, the lines are called x (drawn from left to right, with positive direction to the right of the origin) and y (drawn from bottom to top, with positive direction above the origin). The distance of a point from the lines determine its coordinates and the direction from the origin determines the signs of the coordinates. The standard coordinate plane consists of a plane divided into 4 quadrants by the intersection of two axes, the *x*-axis (horizontal axis) and the *y*-axis (vertical axis).

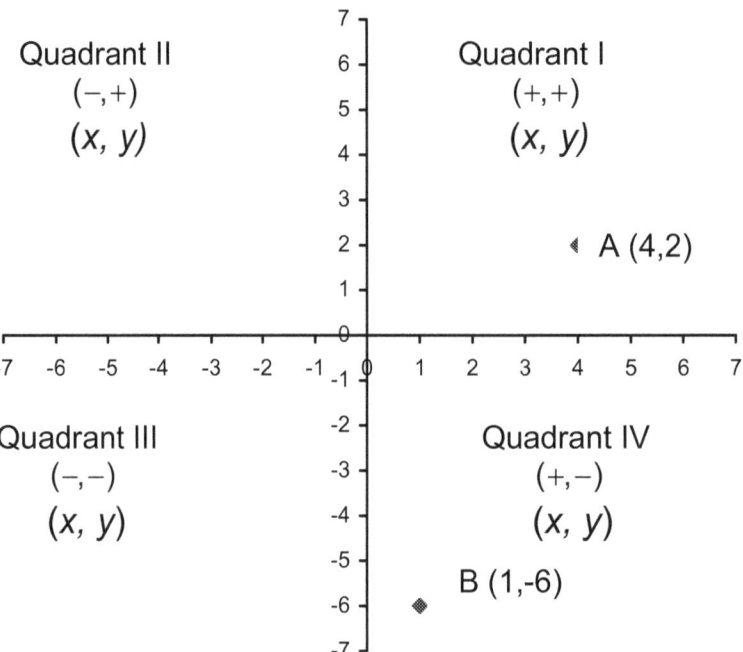

Coordinates - A unique **ordered pair** of numbers that identifies a point on the coordinate plane. The first number in the ordered pair identifies the position with regard to the x-axis while the second number identifies the position in relation to the y-axis (*x* ,*y*).

In the coordinate plane shown above, point A represents the ordered pair (4,2) and point B represents the ordered pair (1,-6).

Slope – The slope of a line is the "slant". A downward left to right slant represents a negative slope. An upward slant is a positive slope.
The formula for calculating the slope of a line with coordinates (x_1, y_1) and (x_2, y_2) is:

$$\text{slope} = \frac{y_2 - y_1}{x_2 - x_1}$$

The top of the fraction represents the change in the y coordinates, it is called the **rise**.

The bottom of the fraction represents the change in the x coordinates, it is called the **run**.

Example: Find the slope of a line with points at (2,2) and (7,8).

$$\frac{(8)-(2)}{(7)-(2)}$$ plug the values into the formula

$$\frac{6}{5}$$ solve the rise over run

$= 1.2$ solve for the slope

The length of a line segment is the **distance** between two different points, A and B. The formula for the length of a line is:

$$\text{length} = \sqrt{(x_1 - x_2)^2 + (y_1 - y_2)^2}$$

Example: Find the length between the points (2,2) and (7,8)

$= \sqrt{(2-7)^2 + (2-8)^2}$ plug the values into the formula

$= \sqrt{(-5)^2 + (-6)^2}$ calculate the x and y differences

$= \sqrt{25 + 36}$ square the values

$= \sqrt{61}$ add the two values

$= 7.81$ calculate the square root

BASIC SKILLS

Skill 3.4 Identify real-world examples that represent geometric concepts including perpendicularity, parallelism, tangency, symmetry, and transformations (e.g., flips, slides, and turns).

Parallel lines or planes do not intersect. Two parallel lines have the same slope.

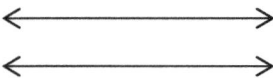

Perpendicular lines or planes form a 90 degree angle to each other. Perpendicular lines have slopes that are negative reciprocals.

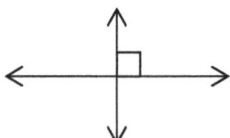

Example: One line passes through the points (-4, -6) and (4, 6) and another line passes through the points (-5, -4) and (3, 8). Are these lines parallel, perpendicular, or neither?

Find the slopes.

$$m = \frac{y_2 - y_1}{x_2 - x_1}$$

$$m_1 = \frac{6-(-6)}{4-(-4)} = \frac{6+6}{4+4} = \frac{12}{8} = \frac{3}{2}$$

$$m_2 = \frac{8-(-4)}{3-(-5)} = \frac{8+4}{3+5} = \frac{12}{8} = \frac{3}{2}$$

Since the slopes are the same, the lines are parallel.

Example: One line passes through the points (1, -3) and (0, -6) and another line passes through the points (4, 1) and (-2, 3). Are these lines parallel, perpendicular, or neither?

Find the slopes.

$$m = \frac{y_2 - y_1}{x_2 - x_1}$$

$$m_1 = \frac{-6-(-3)}{0-1} = \frac{-6+3}{-1} = \frac{-3}{-1} = 3$$

$$m_2 = \frac{3-1}{-2-4} = \frac{2}{-6} = -\frac{1}{3}$$

The slopes are negative reciprocals, so the lines are perpendicular.

Example: One line passes through the points (-2, 4) and (2, 5) and another line passes through the points (-1, 0) and (5, 4). Are these lines parallel, perpendicular, or neither?

Find the slopes.

$$m = \frac{y_2 - y_1}{x_2 - x_1}$$

$$m_1 = \frac{5-4}{2-(-2)} = \frac{1}{2+2} = \frac{1}{4}$$

$$m_2 = \frac{4-0}{5-(-1)} = \frac{4}{5+1} = \frac{4}{6} = \frac{2}{3}$$

Since the slopes are not the same, the lines are not parallel. Since they are not negative reciprocals, they are not perpendicular. Therefore, the answer is "neither."

There are four basic **transformational symmetries**: **translation, rotation, reflection,** and **glide reflection**. The transformation of an object is its image. If the original object was labeled with letters, such as $ABCD$, the image may be labeled with the same letters followed by a prime symbol, $A'B'C'D'$.

A **translation** is a transformation that "slides" an object a fixed distance in a given direction. The original object and its translation have the same shape and size, and they face in the same direction.

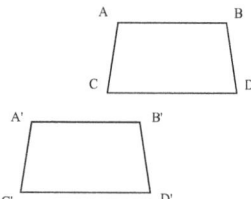

An example of a translation in architecture is stadium seating. The seats are the same size and shape and face in the same direction.

A **rotation** is a transformation that turns a figure about a fixed point called the center of rotation. An object and its rotation are the same shape and size, but the figures may be turned in different directions. Rotations can occur in either a clockwise or a counterclockwise direction.

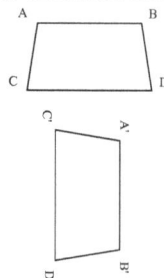

Rotations can be seen in wallpaper and art, and a Ferris wheel is an example of rotation.

An object and its **reflection** have the same shape and size, but the figures face in opposite directions.

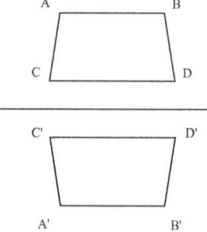

The line (where a mirror may be placed) is called the **line of reflection**. The distance from a point to the line of reflection is the same as the distance from the point's image to the line of reflection.

A **glide reflection** is a combination of a reflection and a translation.

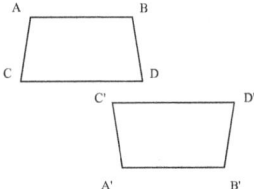

Objects that are **tangent** make contact at a single point or along a line without crossing. Understanding tangency is critical in the construction industry where architects and engineers must figure out how various elements will fit together. An example is the building of a stair railing. The architect must determine the points of tangency between the banisters, which might even be curved, and the posts supporting the banisters.

Many types of flooring found in our homes are examples of **symmetry**: Oriental carpets, tiling, and patterned carpet. The human body is an example of symmetry, even though it is not usually perfect. If you split the torso down the middle, on each half, you will find one ear, one eye, one nostril, one shoulder, one arm, one leg, and so on, in approximately the same place.

TEACHER CERTIFICATION STUDY GUIDE

COMPETENCY 4.0   KNOWLEDGE OF ALGEBRAIC THINKING

Skill 4.1   Analyze and generalize patterns including arithmetic and geometric sequences.

Arithmetic Sequences

When given a set of numbers where the common difference between the terms is constant, use the following formula:

$$a_n = a_1 + (n-1)d$$

where a_1 = the first term
n = the nth term (general term)
d = the common difference

Example: Find the 8th term of the arithmetic sequence 5, 8, 11, 14, ...

$a_n = a_1 + (n-1)d$
$a_n = 5$ identify the 1st term
$d = 8 - 5 = 3$ find d
$a_n = 5 + (8-1)3$ substitute
$a_n = 26$

Example: Given two terms of an arithmetic sequence, find a_1 and d.

$a_4 = 21$ $a_6 = 32$
$a_n = a + (n-1)d$ $a_4 = 21, n = 4$
$21 = a_1 + (4-1)d$ $a_6 = 32, n = 6$
$32 = a_1 + (6-1)d$

$21 = a_1 + 3d$ solve the system of equations
$32 = a_1 + 5d$

$21 = a_1 + 3d$
$-32 = -a_1 - 5d$ multiply by -1
$-11 = -2d$ add the equations
$5.5 = d$

$21 = a_1 + 3(5.5)$ substitute d = 5.5, into one of the equations
$21 = a_1 + 16.5$
$a_1 = 4.5$

The sequence begins with 4.5 and has a common difference of 5.5 between numbers.

BASIC SKILLS

Geometric Sequences

When using geometric sequences, we compare consecutive numbers to find the common ratio.

$$r = \frac{a_{n+1}}{a_n}$$

where r = common ratio
a = the nth term

The ratio is then used in the geometric sequence formula:
$$a_n = a_1 r^{n-1}$$

Example: Find the 8th term of the geometric sequence 2, 8, 32, 128 ...

$r = \frac{a_{n+1}}{a_n}$ use common ratio formula to find ratio

$r = \frac{8}{2}$ substitute $a_n = 2$ $a_{n+1} = 8$

$r = 4$

$a_n = a_1 \bullet r^{n-1}$ use r = 4 to solve for the 8th term

$a_n = 2 \bullet 4^{8-1}$

$a_n = 32{,}768$

Skill 4.2 Interpret algebraic expressions using words, symbols, variables, tables, and graphs.

We use tables, graphs, and rules to represent relationships between two quantities. In this example, the rule y = 9x describes the relationship between the total amount earned, y, and the total amount of $9 sunglasses sold, x.

Number of Sunglasses Sold	1	5	10	15
Total Dollars Earned	9	45	90	135

Each *(x,y)* relationship between a pair of values is a coordinate pair and can be plotted on a graph. The coordinate pairs *(1,9), (5,45), (10,90),* and *(15,135)* are plotted on the graph below.

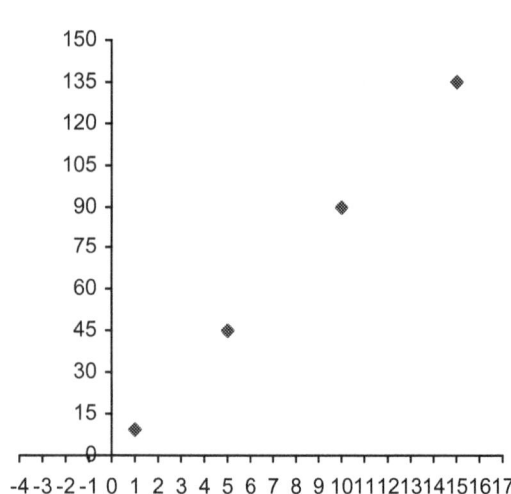

The graph (left) shows a linear relationship. A linear relationship is one in which two quantities are proportional to each other. Doubling x also doubles y. On a graph, a straight line depicts a linear relationship.

We can analyze the function or relationship between two quantities to determine how one quantity depends on the other. For example, the function below shows a relationship between y and x: $y = 2x+1$.

We can analyze the relationship between two or more variables using a table, graph, written description, or symbolic rule. The function, $y = 2x+1$, is a symbolic rule. The table (below) is another representation of the same relationship.

x	0	2	3	6	9
y	1	5	7	13	19

Alternatively, we could describe the relationship in words by saying the value of y is equal to two times the value of x, plus one. Finally, we could show the relationship on a graph by plotting given points such as the ones shown in the table above.

Another way to describe a function is as a process in which one or more numbers are input into an imaginary machine that produces another number as the output. If 5 is the input, x, and the process is $x + 1$, the output, y, will equal 6.

In real situations, we can describe relationships mathematically. We can use the function $y = x+1$ to represent the idea that people age one year on their birthday. To describe the relationship in which a person's monthly medical costs are 6 times a person's age, we could write $y = 6x$. Where y is the monthly medical costs and x is the person's age. We could predict the monthly cost of medical care using this function. A 20 year-old person would spend $120 per month (120 = 20*6). An 80 year-old person would spend $480 per month (480 = 80*6). Thus, one could analyze the relationship to say: as you get older, medical costs increase $6.00 each year.

BASIC SKILLS

TEACHER CERTIFICATION STUDY GUIDE

Skill 4.3   Solve equations and inequalities graphically or algebraically.

Procedure for solving algebraic equations.

Example: $3(x+3) = {}^-2x+4$ Solve for x.

1) Expand to eliminate all parentheses.

   $3x + 9 = {}^-2x + 4$

2) Multiply each term by the LCD to eliminate all denominators.

3) Combine like terms on each side when possible.

4) Use the properties to put all variables on one side and all constants on the other side.

   $\rightarrow 3x + 9 - 9 = {}^-2x + 4 - 9$ (subtract nine from both sides)

   $\rightarrow 3x = {}^-2x - 5$

   $\rightarrow 3x + 2x = {}^-2x + 2x - 5$ (add 2x to both sides)

   $\rightarrow 5x = {}^-5$

   $\rightarrow \dfrac{5x}{5} = \dfrac{{}^-5}{5}$ (divide both sides by 5)

   $\rightarrow x = {}^-1$

Example: Solve: $3(2x+5) - 4x = 5(x+9)$

$6x + 15 - 4x = 5x + 45$
$2x + 15 = 5x + 45$
${}^-3x + 15 = 45$
${}^-3x = 30$
$x = {}^-10$

BASIC SKILLS

Example: Mark and Mike are twins. Three times Mark's age plus four equals four times Mike's age minus 14. How old are the boys?

Since the boys are twins, their ages are the same. "Translate" the English into Algebra. Let x = their age

$3x + 4 = 4x - 14$

$18 = x$

The boys are each 18 years old.

The solution **set of linear equations** is all the ordered pairs of real numbers that satisfy both equations, thus the intersection of the lines There are two methods for solving linear equations: **linear combinations** and **substitution**.

In the **substitution** method, an equation is solved for either variable. Then, that solution is substituted in the other equation to find the remaining variable.

Example:
(1) $2x + 8y = 4$
(2) $x - 3y = 5$

(2a) $x = 3y + 5$ Solve equation (2) for x

(1a) $2(3y + 5) + 8y = 4$ Substitute x in equation (1)
$6y + 10 + 8y = 4$ Solve.
$14y = -6$
$y = \frac{-3}{7}$ Solution

(2) $x - 3y = 5$
$x - 3(\frac{-3}{7}) = 5$ Substitute the value of y.
$x = \frac{26}{7} = 3\frac{5}{7}$ Solution

Thus the solution set of the system of equations is $(3\frac{5}{7}, \frac{-3}{7})$.

In the **linear combinations** method, one or both of the equations are replaced with an equivalent equation in order that the two equations can be combined (added or subtracted) to eliminate one variable.

Example: (1) $4x + 3y = -2$
          (2) $5x - y = 7$

          (1) $4x + 3y = -2$
          (2a) $15x - 3y = 21$ Multiply equation (2) by 3

          $19x = 19$ Combining (1) and (2a)
          $x = 1$ Solve.

To find y, substitute the value of x in equation 1 (or 2).
          (1) $4x + 3y = -2$
               $4(1) + 3y = -2$
               $4 + 3y = -2$
               $3y = -2$
               $y = -2$

Thus the solution is $x = 1$ and $y = -2$ or the order pair (1, -2).

Example: Solve for x and y.

$4x + 6y = 340$
$3x + 8y = 360$

To solve by addition-subtraction:

Multiply the first equation by 4: $4(4x + 6y = 340)$

Multiply the other equation by $^-3$: $^-3(3x + 8y = 360)$

By doing this, the equations can be added to each other to eliminate one variable and solve for the other variable.

$$16x + 24y = 1360$$
$$\underline{-9x - 24y = {}^-1080}$$
$$7x = 280$$
$$x = 40$$

solving for y, $y = 30$

TEACHER CERTIFICATION STUDY GUIDE

Procedure for solving algebraic inequalities

We use the same procedure used for solving linear equations, but the answer is represented in graphical form on the number line or in interval form.

Example: Solve the inequality, show its solution using interval form, and graph the solution on the number line.

$$\frac{5x}{8} + 3 \geq 2x - 5$$

$$8\left(\frac{5x}{8}\right) + 8(3) \geq 8(2x) - 5(8) \qquad \text{Multiply by LCD = 8.}$$

$$5x + 24 \geq 16x - 40$$

$$5x + 24 - 24 - 16x \geq 16x - 16x - 40 - 24$$
Subtract 16x and 24 from both sides of the equation.

$$^-11x \geq\, ^-64$$

$$\frac{^-11x}{^-11} \leq \frac{^-64}{^-11}$$

$$x \leq \frac{64}{11} \; ; \; x \leq 5\frac{9}{11}$$

Solution in interval form: $\left(^-\infty, 5\frac{9}{11}\right]$

Note: "] " means $5\frac{9}{11}$ is included in the solution.

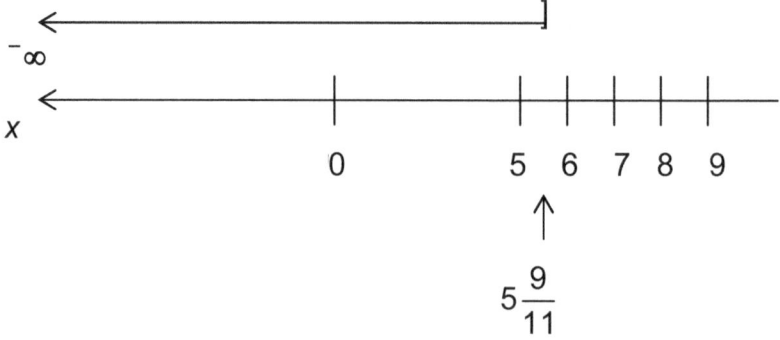

BASIC SKILLS

Example: Solve the following inequality and express your answer in both interval and graphical form.

$$3x - 8 < 2(3x - 1)$$

$$3x - 8 < 6x - 2 \qquad \text{Distributive property.}$$

$$3x - 6x - 8 + 8 < 6x - 6x - 2 + 8$$

Add 8 and subtract 6x from both sides of the equation.

$$^-3x < 6$$

$$\frac{^-3x}{^-3} > \frac{6}{^-3} \qquad \text{Note the change in direction of the equality.}$$

$$x > ^-2$$

Graphical form: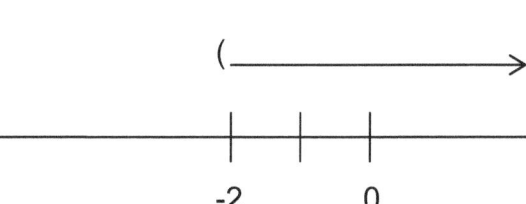

or

Interval form: $(^-2, \infty)$

Recall that using a parentheses or an open circle implies the point in not included in the answer and using a bracket or a closed circle implies the point is included in the answer.

Example: Solve: $6x + 21 < 8x + 31$

$$^-2x + 21 < 31$$
$$^-2x < 10$$
$$x > ^-5$$

Note that the inequality sign has changed.

BASIC SKILLS

Graphically

A first degree equation has an equation of the form $ax + by = c$. To find the slope of a line, solve the equation for y. This gets the equation into **slope intercept form**, $y = mx + b$. **m is the line's slope.**

The y-intercept is the coordinate of the point where a line crosses the y axis. To find the y intercept, substitute 0 for x and solve for y. This is the y-intercept. In slope intercept form, $y = mx + b$, b is the y-intercept.

To find the x intercept, substitute 0 for y and solve for x. This is the x-intercept.

If the equation solves to **x = any number**, then the graph is a **vertical line**. It only has an x-intercept. Its slope is **undefined**.

If the equation solves to **y = any number**, then the graph is a **horizontal line**. It only has a y-intercept. Its slope is 0 (zero).

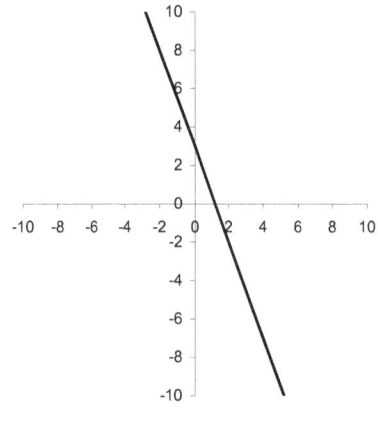

$$5x + 2y = 6$$
$$y = {}^-5/2\,x + 3$$

We can find the equation of a line from its graph by finding its slope (see Skill 3.2 for the slope formula) and its y-intercept.

$$Y - y_a = m(X - x_a)$$

(x_a, y_a) can be (x_1, y_1) or (x_2, y_2). If we distribute **m**, the value of the slope, through the parentheses, we can rewrite the equation into other forms.

Example: Find the equation of a line through $(9, {}^-6)$ and $({}^-1, 2)$.

$$\text{slope} = \frac{y_2 - y_1}{x_2 - x_1} = \frac{2 - {}^-6}{{}^-1 - 9} = \frac{8}{{}^-10} = -\frac{4}{5}$$

$$Y - y_a = m(X - x_a) \to Y - 2 = {}^-4/5(X - {}^-1) \to$$
$$Y - 2 = {}^-4/5(X + 1) \to Y - 2 = {}^-4/5\, X - 4/5 \to$$
$$Y = {}^-4/5\, X + 6/5 \quad \text{This is the slope-intercept form.}$$

Multiplying by 5 to eliminate fractions, it is:

$$5Y = {}^-4X + 6 \to 4X + 5Y = 6 \quad \text{Standard form.}$$

Example: Find the slope and intercepts of $3x + 2y = 14$.

$$3x + 2y = 14$$
$$2y = {}^-3x + 14$$
$$y = {}^-3/2\, x + 7$$

The slope of the line is ${}^-3/2$. The y-intercept of the line is 7.

We can also find the intercepts by substituting 0 in place of the other variable in the equation.

To find the y intercept:
let $x = 0$; $3(0) + 2y = 14$
$0 + 2y = 14$
$2y = 14$
$y = 7$
$(0, 7)$ is the y-intercept.

To find the x intercept:
let $y = 0$; $3x + 2(0) = 14$
$3x + 0 = 14$
$3x = 14$
$x = 14/3$
$(14/3, 0)$ is the x-intercept.

Example: Sketch the graph of the line represented by $2x + 3y = 6$.

Let $x = 0 \rightarrow 2(0) + 3y = 6$
$\rightarrow 3y = 6$
$\rightarrow y = 2$
$\rightarrow (0, 2)$ is the y-intercept.

Let $y = 0 \rightarrow 2x + 3(0) = 6$
$\rightarrow 2x = 6$
$\rightarrow x = 3$
$\rightarrow (3, 0)$ is the x-intercept.

Let $x = 1 \rightarrow 2(1) + 3y = 6$
$\rightarrow 2 + 3y = 6$
$\rightarrow 3y = 4$
$\rightarrow y = \dfrac{4}{3}$
$\rightarrow \left(1, \dfrac{4}{3}\right)$ is the third point.

Plotting the three points on the coordinate system, we get the following:

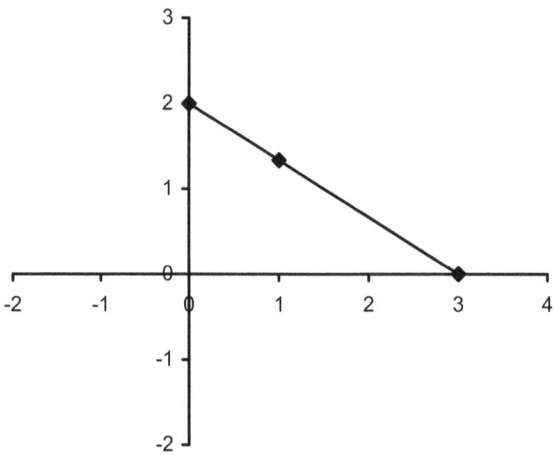

To graph an inequality, solve the inequality for y. This gets the inequality in **slope-intercept form**, (for example: **y** < m**x** + b). The point (0,b) is the *y*-intercept and m is the line's slope.

If the inequality solves to **x** ≥ **any number**, then the graph includes a **vertical line**.

If the inequality solves to **y ≤ any number**, then the graph includes a **horizontal line**.

When graphing a linear inequality, the line is dotted if the inequality sign is < or >. If the inequality signs are either ≥ or ≤, the line on the graph is solid. Shade above the line when the inequality sign is ≥ or >. Shade below the line when the inequality sign is < or ≤. For inequalities of the forms $x >$ number, $x \leq$ number, $x <$ number, or $x \geq$ number, draw a vertical line (solid or dotted). Shade to the right for > or ≥. Shade to the left for < or ≤.

Remember: **Dividing or multiplying by a negative number will reverse the direction of the inequality sign.**

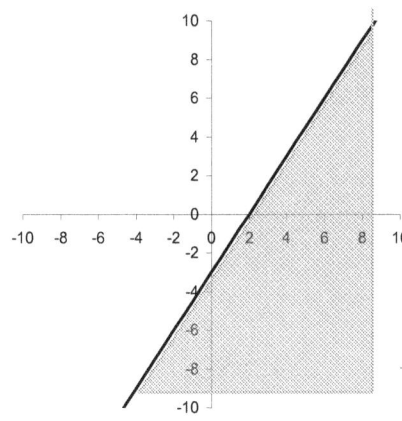

$$3x - 2y \geq 6$$
$$y \leq 3/2\, x - 3$$

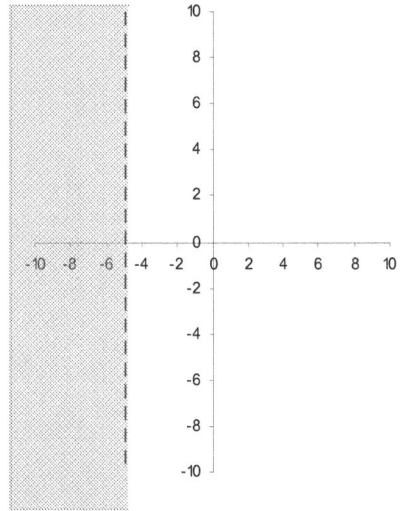

$$3x + 12 < -3$$
$$x < {}^-5$$

BASIC SKILLS

Example: Solve by graphing:

$x + y \leq 6$
$x - 2y \leq 6$

Solving the inequalities for y, they become:

$y \leq {}^-x + 6$ (y-intercept of 6 and slope = $^-1$)
$y \geq 1/2\,x - 3$ (y-intercept of $^-3$ and slope = $1/2$)

A graph with shading is shown below:

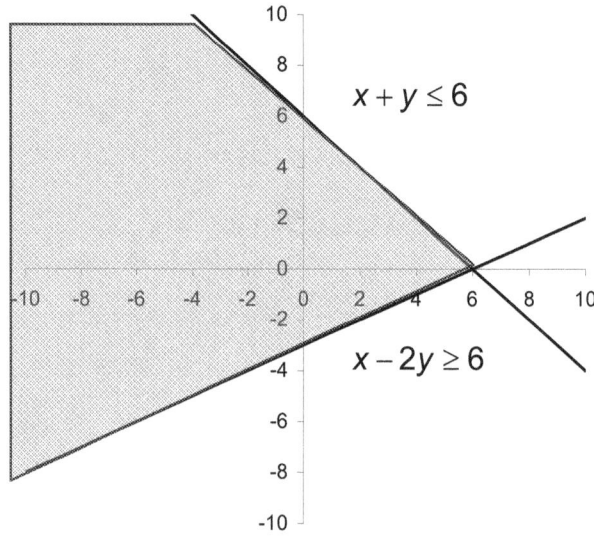

TEACHER CERTIFICATION STUDY GUIDE

Real World Example Problems

Example: Mark and Mike are twins. Three times Mark's age plus four equals four times Mike's age minus 14. How old are the boys?

Since the boys are twins, their ages are the same. "Translate" the English into Algebra. Let x = their age

$3x + 4 = 4x - 14$

$18 = x$

The boys are each 18 years old.

Example: The YMCA wants to sell raffle tickets to raise $32,000. If they must pay $7,250 in expenses and prizes out of the money collected from the tickets, how many tickets worth $25 each must they sell?

Let x = number of tickets sold
Then $25x$ = total money collected for x tickets

Total money minus expenses is greater than $32,000.

$25x - 7250 = 32,000$
$25x = 39350$
$x = 1570$

If they sell 1,570 tickets, they will raise $32,000.

Example: The Simpsons went out for dinner. All 4 of them ordered the aardvark steak dinner. Bert paid for the 4 meals and included a tip of $12 for a total of $84.60. How much was an aardvark steak dinner?

Let x = the price of one aardvark dinner
So $4x$ = the price of 4 aardvark dinners
$4x = 84.60 - 12$
$4x = 72.60$
$x = \dfrac{72.60}{4} = \$18.15$ The price of one aardvark dinner.

BASIC SKILLS

Some word problems can be solved using a system (group) of equations or inequalities. Watch for words like greater than, less than, at least, or no more than which indicate the need for inequalities.

Example: Farmer Greenjeans bought 4 cows and 6 sheep for $1700. Mr. Ziffel bought 3 cows and 12 sheep for $2400. If all the cows were the same price and all the sheep were another price, find the price charged for a cow or for a sheep.

Let x = price of a cow
Let y = price of a sheep

Then Farmer Greenjeans' equation would be: $4x + 6y = 1700$
Mr. Ziffel's equation would be: $3x + 12y = 2400$

To solve by **addition-subtraction**:
Multiply the first equation by $^-2$: $^-2(4x + 6y = 1700)$
Keep the other equation the same: $(3x + 12y = 2400)$
By doing this, the equations can be added to each other to eliminate one variable and solve for the other variable.

$$^-8x - 12y = ^-3400$$
$$\underline{3x + 12y = 2400} \quad \text{Add these equations.}$$
$$^-5x \quad\quad = ^-1000$$

$x = 200 \leftarrow$ the price of a cow was $200.
Solving for y, $y = 150 \leftarrow$ the price of a sheep, $150.

To solve by **substitution**:

Solve one of the equations for a variable. (Try to make an equation without fractions if possible.) Substitute this expression into the equation that you have not yet used. Solve the resulting equation for the value of the remaining variable.

$$4x + 6y = 1700$$
$$3x + 12y = 2400 \leftarrow \text{Solve this equation for } x.$$

BASIC SKILLS

It becomes $x = 800 - 4y$. Now substitute $800 - 4y$ in place of x in the OTHER equation. $4x + 6y = 1700$ now becomes:

$$4(800 - 4y) + 6y = 1700$$
$$3200 - 16y + 6y = 1700$$
$$3200 - 10y = 1700$$
$$^-10y = {}^-1500$$

$y = 150$, or $150 for a sheep.

Substituting 150 back into an equation for y, find x.
$$4x + 6(150) = 1700$$
$$4x + 900 = 1700$$
$$4x = 800 \text{ so } x = 200 \text{ for a cow.}$$

Example: Sharon's Bike Shoppe can assemble a 3 speed bike in 30 minutes or a 10 speed bike in 60 minutes. The profit on each bike sold is $60 for a 3 speed or $75 for a 10 speed bike. How many of each type of bike should they assemble during an 8 hour day (480 minutes) to make the maximum profit? Total daily profit must be at least $300.

Let x = number of 3 speed bikes.
y = number of 10 speed bikes.

Since there are only 480 minutes to use each day,

$30x + 60y \leq 480$ is the first inequality.

Since the total daily profit must be at least $300,

$60x + 75y \geq 300$ is the second inequality.

$30x + 60y \leq 480$ solves to $y \leq 8 - 1/2\,x$
$$60y \leq -30x + 480$$
$$y \leq -\frac{1}{2}x + 8$$

$60x + 75y \geq 300$ solves to $y \geq 4 - 4/5\,x$
$$75y + 60x \geq 300$$
$$75y \geq -60x + 300$$
$$y \geq -\frac{4}{5}x + 4$$

This problem can be solved by graphing these two inequalities.

Graph these 2 inequalities:

$$y \leq 8 - 1/2\, x$$
$$y \geq 4 - 4/5\, x$$

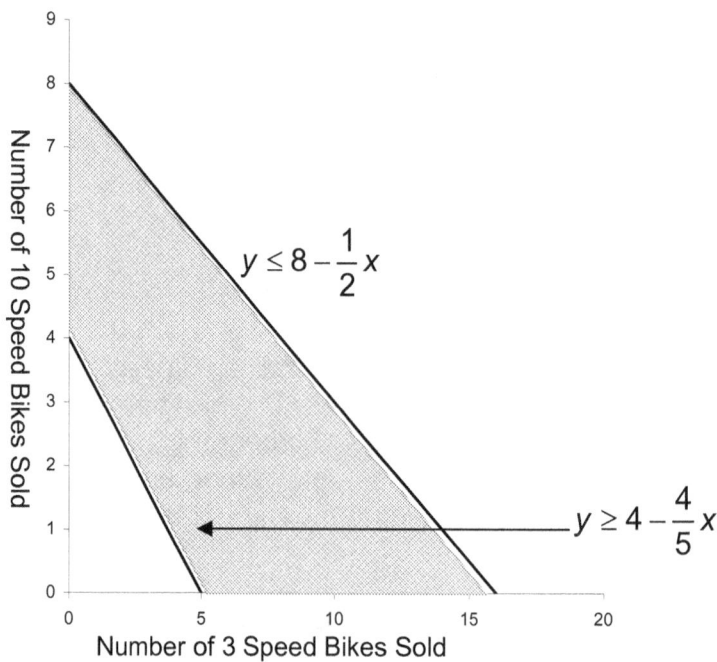

Realize that $x \geq 0$ and $y \geq 0$, since the number of bikes assembled can not be a negative number. Graph these as additional constraints on the problem. The number of bikes assembled must always be an integer value, so points within the shaded area of the graph must have integer values. The maximum profit will occur at or near a corner of the shaded portion of this graph. Those points occur at (0,4), (0,8), (16,0), or (5,0).

Since profits are $60/3-speed or $75/10-speed, the profit would be :

(0,4) $60(0) + 75(4) = 300$
(0,8) $60(0) + 75(8) = 600$
(16,0) $60(16) + 75(0) = 960$ ← Maximum profit
(5,0) $60(5) + 75(0) = 300$

The maximum profit would occur if 16 3-speed bikes are made daily.

TEACHER CERTIFICATION STUDY GUIDE

Skill 4.4 Determine whether a number or ordered pair is among the solutions of given equations or inequalities.

If substituting a value for the variable results in the Left Hand Side = Right Hand Side or a true statement, then the value is the solution for that equation.

Example: $2x = 6$
(LHS) (RHS)

This statement is only true if we substitute 3 for x.
$2 \times 3 = 6$ (True).

Therefore, 3 is a solution for the equation.

Example: Is 2 a solution of $2x - 6 = 6x + 1$?

Substituting 2 for x:

$2(2) - 6 = 6(2) + 1 \rightarrow 4 - 6 = 12 + 1 \rightarrow {}^-2 = 13$ (False)

Therefore, 2 is not a solution.

Example: Is the ordered pair (2, 3) a solution to the linear equation $y = 5x - 3$?

Substituting 2 for x and 3 for y:

$3 = 5(2) - 3$
$3 = 10 - 3$
$3 = 7$

No, (2,3) is not among the solutions of the equation.

Example: Is the ordered pair (-4,-2) a solution to the inequality $y \leq 2x + 6$?

Substituting -4 for x and -2 for y

$-2 \leq 2(-4) + 6$
$-2 \leq -8 + 6$
$-2 \leq -2$

Yes, (-4, -2) is among the solutions of the inequality.

TEACHER CERTIFICATION STUDY GUIDE

COMPETENCY 5.0 KNOWLEDGE OF DATA ANALYSIS AND PROBABILITY

Skill 5.1 Analyze data and solve problems using data presented in histograms, bar graphs, circle graphs, pictographs, tables, and charts.

To make a **bar graph** or a **pictograph**, determine the scale to use for the graph. Then determine the length of each bar on the graph or determine the number of pictures needed to represent each item of information. Be sure to include an explanation of the scale in the legend.

Example: A class had the following grades:
4 A's, 9 B's, 8 C's, 1 D, 3 F's.
Graph these on a bar graph and a pictograph.

Pictograph

Grade	Number of Students
A	☺☺☺☺
B	☺☺☺☺☺☺☺☺☺
C	☺☺☺☺☺☺☺☺
D	☺
F	☺☺☺

Bar graph

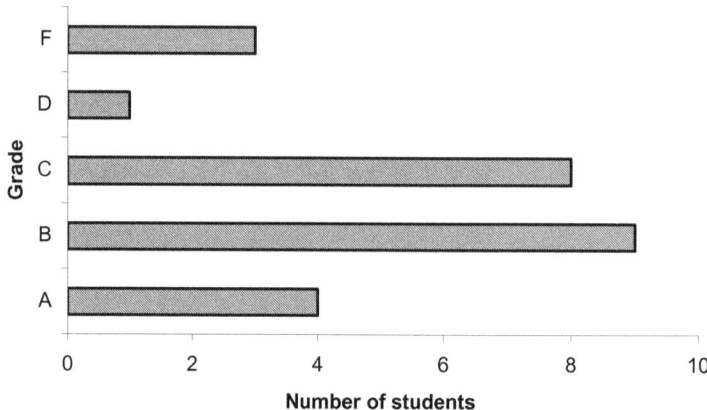

To make a **line graph**, determine appropriate scales for both the vertical and horizontal axes (based on the information). Describe what each axis represents and mark the scale periodically on each axis. Graph the individual points of the graph and connect the points on the graph from left to right.

Example: Graph the following information using a line graph.

The number of National Merit finalists per school per year

	90-91	91-92	92-93	93-94	94-95	95-96
Central	3	5	1	4	6	8
Wilson	4	2	3	2	3	2

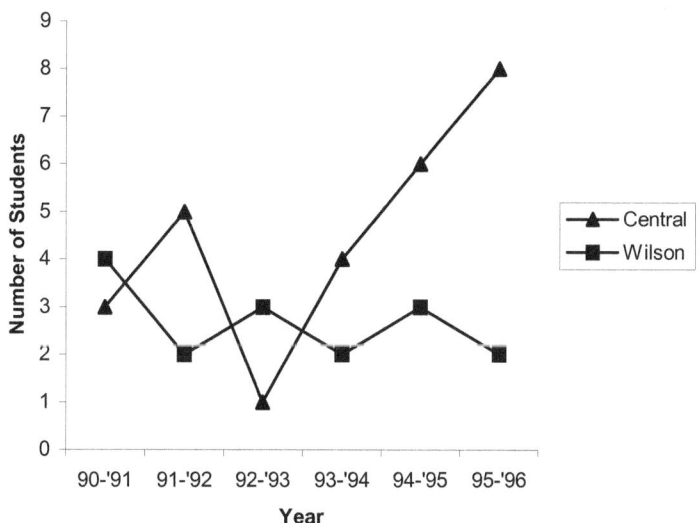

To make a **circle graph**, total all the information. Determine the central angle to use for each sector of the graph using the following formula:

$$\frac{\text{information}}{\text{total information}} \times 360° = \text{degrees in central } \angle$$

Lay out the central angles to match these sizes, label each section, and include its percent.

Example: Graph this information on a circle graph:

Monthly expenses:

Rent, $400
Food, $150
Utilities, $75
Clothes, $75
Church, $100
Misc., $200

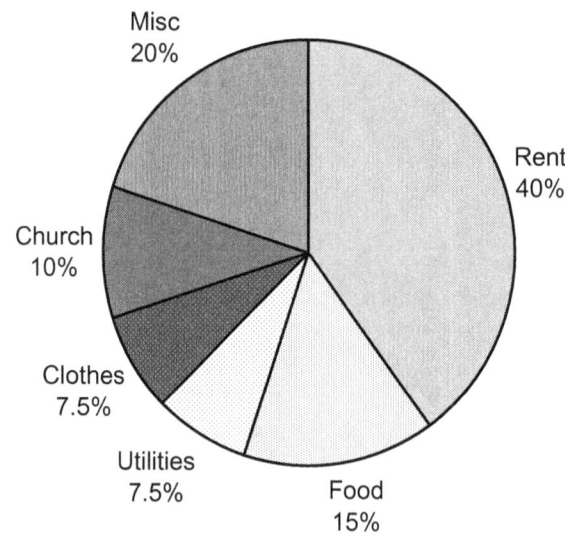

Histograms summarize information from large sets of data that can be naturally grouped into intervals. The vertical axis indicates **frequency** (the number of times any particular data value occurs), and the horizontal axis indicates data values or ranges of data values. The number of data values in any interval is the **frequency of the interval**.

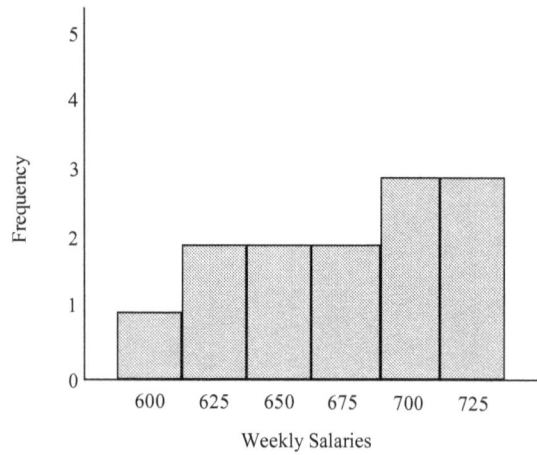

BASIC SKILLS

Skill 5.2   **Identify how the presentation of data can lead to different or inappropriate interpretations.**

Pictographs can be misleading, especially if drawn to represent 3-dimensional objects. If two or more dimensions are changed in reflecting ratio, the overall visual effect can be misinterpreted. Bar and line graphs can be misleading if the scales are changed, e.g., using relatively small scale increments for large numbers will make the comparison differences seem much greater than if larger scale increments are used. Circle graphs, or pie charts, are excellent for comparing relative amounts. However, they cannot be used to represent absolute amounts, and if interpreted as such, they are misleading.

Skill 5.3   **Calculate range, mean, median, and mode(s) from sets of data and interpret the meaning of the measures of central tendency (i.e., mean, median, and mode) and dispersion (i.e., range and standard deviation).**

The arithmetic **mean** (or average) of a set of numbers is the *sum* of the numbers given, *divided* by the number of items in the set.

Example: Find the mean of the following numbers. Round to the nearest tenth.

24.6, 57.3, 44.1, 39.8, 64.5

The sum is 230.3

The mean is 230.3/5

= 46.06, rounded to 46.1 (nearest tenth)

The **median** of a set is the middle number. To calculate the median, we must arrange the terms in order. If there are an even number of terms, the median is the mean of the two middle terms.

Example: Find the median.

12. 14. 27. 3. 13. 7. 17. 12. 22. 6. 16

Rearrange the terms.
3, 6, 7, 12, 12, 13, 14, 16, 17, 22, 27

Since there are 11 numbers, the middle would be the sixth number or 13.

The **mode** of a set of numbers is the number that occurs with the greatest frequency. A set can have no mode if each term appears exactly one time. Similarly, there can also be more than one mode.

Example: Find the mode.

26, 15, 37, **26**, 35, **26**, 15

15 appears twice, but 26 appears 3 times, therefore the mode is 26.

The **range** is the difference between the highest and lowest values in the data set.

Example: Given the ungrouped data below, calculate the mean and range.

15 22 28 25 34 38
18 25 30 33 19 23

Mean (X) = 25.8333333
Range: 38 − 15 = 23
standard deviation (σ) = 6.699137
Variance (σ^2) = 48.87879

The **variance** is the sum of the squares divided by the number of items. (the lower case greek letter sigma squared (σ^2) represents variance).

$$\frac{Sx^2}{N} = \sigma^2$$

The larger the value of the variance the larger the spread

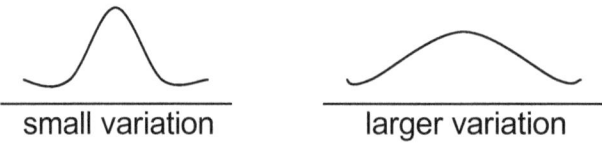

small variation   larger variation

Standard deviation is the square root of the variance. The lower case Greek letter sigma (σ) is used to represent standard deviation.

$$\sigma = \sqrt{\sigma^2}$$

Most statistical calculators have standard deviation keys on them and should be used when asked to calculate statistical functions. It is important to become familiar with the calculator and the location of the necessary keys.

BASIC SKILLS

Skill 5.4 Identify how the measures of central tendency (i.e., mean, median, or mode) can lead to different interpretations

Different situations require different information. Information can be misleading if the data is not presented appropriately. If a data set contains one very high or very low value, the mean will not be representative. For example, including the teacher's height in the mean height of a classroom. If the data clusters around two numbers with a large gap between them, the median will not be representative. For example, expressing the median height in a family of two parents and two small children. Modes are best used with categorical data. In other words, do not mix apples with oranges. For example, a mode of the sale of men's shoe sizes would be helpful to a store when reordering stock of men's shoes. However, finding the mode of men and women's shoe sizes combined would not be a good indicator of the stock that should be reordered.

Consider the set of test scores from a math class: 0, 16, 19, 65, 65, 65, 68, 69, 70, 72, 73, 73, 75, 78, 80, 85, 88, and 92. The mean is 64.06 and the median is 71. Since there are only three scores less than the mean out of the eighteen score, the median (71) is a more descriptive score.

Example: Is the mean, median, or mode the best measure of central tendency for the set 135, 135, 137, 190?

The mean is 149.25, the median is 136, and the mode is 135. Thus, the median or mode are better measures than the mean since they are both closer to the majority of the scores.

Example: The yearly salaries of the employees of Company A are $11,000, $12,000, $12,000, $15,000, $20,000, and $25,000. Which measure of central tendency would you use if you were a manager? If you were an employee trying to get a raise?

The mean is $15,833 The median is $13,500 The mode is $12,000
The manager would probably use the mean since it is the largest amount.
The employee would most likely use the mode since is the smallest.

Skill 5.5 Calculate the probability of a specified outcome.

In probability, the **sample space** is a list of all possible outcomes of an experiment. For example, the sample space of tossing two coins is the set {HH, HT, TT, TH}, the sample space of rolling a six-sided die is the set {1, 2, 3, 4, 5, 6}, and the sample space of measuring the height of students in a class is the set of all real numbers {R}. **Probability** measures the chances of an event occurring. The probability of an event that *must* occur, a certain event, is **one**. When no outcome is favorable, the probability of an impossible event is **zero**.

$$P(\text{event}) = \frac{\text{number of favorable outcomes}}{\text{number of possible outcomes}}$$

Example: Given one die with faces numbered 1 - 6, the probability of tossing an even number on one throw of the die is 3/6 or ½ since there are 3 favorable outcomes (even-numbered faces) and a total of 6 possible outcomes (faces).

Example: We roll a fair die...

a) Find the probability of rolling an even number
b) Find the probability of rolling a number less than three

a) The sample space is S = {1, 2, 3, 4, 5, 6} and the event is the possible even numbers E = {2, 4, 6}.

Hence, the probability of rolling an even number is

$$p(E) = \frac{n(E)}{n(S)} = \frac{3}{6} = \frac{1}{2} \text{ or } 0.5$$

b) A = {1, 2} represents the event of rolling a number less than three.

Hence, the probability of rolling a number less than three is

$$p(A) = \frac{n(A)}{n(S)} = \frac{2}{6} = \frac{1}{3} \text{ or } 0.33$$

Example: A class has thirty students. Of the thirty students, twenty-four are males. Assuming all the students have the same chance of selection, find the probability of selecting a female. (We only select one person.)

The number of females in the class is

$$30 - 24 = 6$$

Hence, the probability of selecting a female is

$$p(female) = \frac{6}{30} = \frac{1}{5} \text{ or } 0.2$$

If A and B are **independent** events then the outcome of event A does not affect the outcome of event B or vice versa. We use the multiplication to find joint probability.

$$P(A \text{ and } B) = P(A) \times P(B)$$

Example: The probability that a patient is allergic to aspirin is .30. If the probability of a patient having a window in his/her room is .40, find the probability that the patient is allergic to aspirin and has a window in his/her room.

Defining the events: A = The patient is allergic to aspirin.
B = The patient has a window in his/her room.

Events A and B are independent, hence
$p(A \text{ and } B) = p(A) \cdot p(B)$
$= (.30)(.40)$
$= .12$ or 12%

Example: Given a jar containing 10 marbles, 3 red, 5 black, and 2 white. What is the probability of drawing a red marble and then a white marble if we return the marble to the jar after choosing?

3/10 X 2/10 = 6/100 = 3/50 or 0.06 or 6%

When the outcome of the first event affects the outcome of the second event, the events are **dependent**. Any two events that are not independent are dependent. This is also known as conditional probability.

$$\text{Probability of (A and B)} = P(A) \times P(B \text{ given } A)$$

BASIC SKILLS

Example: We draw two cards from a deck of 52 cards, without replacement. In other words, we do not return the first card we select to the deck before drawing the second card. What is the probability of drawing two diamonds?

A = drawing a diamond first
B = drawing a diamond second
P(A) = drawing a diamond first
P(B) = drawing a diamond second

P(A) = 13/52 = 1/4   P(B) = 12/52 = 4/17

(PA+B) = 1/4 X 14/17 = 7/34

Example: A class of ten students has six males and four females. If we select two students to represent the class, find the probability that

a) the first is a male and the second is a female.
b) the first is a female and the second is a male.
c) both are females.
d) both are males.

Define the events:

F = a female is selected to represent the class
M = a male is selected to represent the class
F/M = a female is selected after a male has been selected
M/F = a male is selected after a female has been selected

a) Since F and M are dependent events, it follows that
P(M and F) = P(M) · P(F/M)

$$= \frac{6}{10} \times \frac{4}{9} = \frac{3}{5} \times \frac{4}{9} = \frac{12}{45}$$

$P(F/M) = \frac{4}{9}$ instead of , $\frac{4}{10}$ since the selection of a male first changed the sample space from ten to nine students.

b) P(F and M) = P(F) · P(M/F)
$$= \frac{4}{10} \times \frac{6}{9} = \frac{2}{5} \times \frac{2}{3} = \frac{4}{15}$$

c) $P(F \text{ and } F) = p(F) \cdot p(F/F)$
$= \dfrac{4}{10} \times \dfrac{3}{9} = \dfrac{2}{5} \times \dfrac{1}{3} = \dfrac{2}{15}$

d) $P(\text{both are males}) = p(M \text{ and } M)$
$= \dfrac{6}{10} \times \dfrac{5}{9} = \dfrac{30}{90} = \dfrac{1}{3}$

Odds are the ratio of the number of favorable outcomes to the number of unfavorable outcomes. The sum of the favorable outcomes and the unfavorable outcomes will always equal the total possible outcomes. For example, given a bag of 12 red and 7 green marbles compute the odds of randomly selecting a red marble.

$$\text{Odds of red} = \dfrac{12}{19}$$

$$\text{Odds of not getting red} = \dfrac{7}{19}$$

In the case of flipping a coin, it is equally likely that the coin will land on heads or tails. Thus, the odds of tossing a head are 1:1. This is even odds.

Skill 5.6   **Solve and interpret real-world problems involving probability using counting procedures, tables, tree diagrams, and the concepts of permutations and combination**

Counting Procedures
So far, in all the problems we dealt with, we were given the sample space or we could easily obtain it. However, in many real life situations, the sample space and events within it are very large and difficult to find.

There are three techniques to help us find the number of elements in one event or a sample space: counting principle, permutations, and combinations.

The Counting Principle
In a sequence of two distinct events in which the first one has n number of outcomes or possibilities and the second one has m number of outcomes or possibilities, the total number or possibilities of the sequence is

$$n \cdot m$$

Example: A car dealership has three Mazda models and each model comes in a choice of four colors. How many Mazda cars are available at the dealership?

Number of available Mazda cars = (3)(4) = 12

Example: If a license plate consists of three digits followed by three letters, find the possible number of licenses if

a) repetition of letters and digits is **not** allowed

b) repetition of letters and digits is allowed

a) Since there are twenty-six letters and ten digits, using the counting principle, we get

possible # of licenses = (26)(25)(24)(10)(9)(8)

= 11,232,000

b) Since repetitions are allowed, we get

possible # of licenses = (26)(26)(26)(10)(10)(10)

= 17,576,000

The Addition Principle of Counting

If A and B are events, $n(A or B) = n(A) + n(B) - n(A \cap B)$.

Example: In how many ways can you select a black card or a jack from an ordinary deck of playing cards?

Let B denote the set of black cards and let J denote the set of Jacks. Then, $n(B) = 26, n(J) = 4, n(B \cap J) = 2$ and

$$n(B or J) = n(B) + n(J) - n(B \cap A)$$
$$= 26 + 4 - 2$$
$$= 28.$$

The Addition Principle of Counting for Mutually Exclusive Events

If A and B are mutually exclusive events, $n(AorB) = n(A) + n(B)$.

Example: A travel agency offers 40 possible trips: 14 to Asia, 16 to Europe, and 10 to South America. In how many ways can you select a trip to Asia or Europe through this agency?

Let A denote trips to Asia and let E denote trips to Europe. Then, $A \cap E = \emptyset$ and $n(AorE) = 14 + 16 = 30$.

Therefore, the number of ways you can select a trip to Asia or Europe is 30.

The Multiplication Principle of Counting for Dependent Events states:

Let A be a set of outcomes of Stage 1 and B a set of outcomes of Stage 2. Then the number of ways $n(AandB)$, that A and B can occur in a two-stage experiment is given by: $n(AandB) = n(A)n(B|A)$,

where $n(B|A)$ denotes the number of ways B can occur given that A has already occurred.

Example: How many ways from an ordinary deck of 52 cards can two Jacks be drawn in succession if the first card is drawn but not replaced in the deck and then the second card is drawn?

This is a two-stage experiment for which we wish to compute $n(AandB)$, where A is the set of outcomes for which a Jack is obtained on the first draw and B is the set of outcomes for which a Jack is obtained on the second draw.

If the first card drawn is a Jack, then there are only three remaining Jacks left to choose from on the second draw. Thus, drawing two cards without replacement means the events A and B are dependent. $n(AandB) = n(A)n(B|A) = 4 \cdot 3 = 12$

The Multiplication Principle of Counting for Independent Events

Let A be a set of outcomes of Stage 1 and B a set of outcomes of Stage 2. If A and B are independent events then the number of ways $n(A \text{ and } B)$, that A and B can occur in a two-stage experiment is given by: $n(A \text{ and } B) = n(A)n(B)$.

Example: How many six-letter code "words" can be formed if repetition of letters is not allowed?

Since these are code words, a word does not have to look like a word. For example, abcdef could be a code word. Since we must choose a first letter *and* a second letter *and* a third letter *and* a fourth letter *and* a fifth letter *and* a sixth letter, this experiment has six stages.

Since repetition is not allowed there are 26 choices for the first letter; 25 for the second; 24 for the third; 23 for the fourth; 22 for the fifth; and 21 for the sixth. Therefore, we have:

n(six-letter code words without repetition of letters)

$$= 26 \cdot 25 \cdot 24 \cdot 23 \cdot 22 \cdot 21$$

$$= 165,765,600$$

Permutations

In order to understand **Permutations**, we must first address the concept of factorials.

n factorial, written n!, is represented by n! = n(n-1)(n-2) . . . . . (2)(1)

5! = (5)(4)(3)(2)(1) = 120

3! = 3(2)(1) = 6

By definition: 0! = 1
1! = 1

$$\frac{6!}{6!} = 1 \text{ but } \frac{6!}{2!} \neq 3!$$

$$\frac{6!}{2!} = \frac{6 \cdot 5 \cdot 4 \cdot 3 \cdot 2!}{2!} = 6 \cdot 5 \cdot 4 \cdot 3 = 360$$

The number of permutations represents the number of ways we can select r items from n items and arrange them in a specific order. We write permutations as $_nP_r$ and calculate them using the following relationship.

$$_nP_r = \frac{n!}{(n-r)!}$$

When calculating permutations order counts. For example, 2, 3, 4 and 4, 3, 2 are counted as two different permutations. Calculating the number of permutations is not valid with experiments where replacement is allowed.

Example: How many different ways can a president and a vice-president be selected from a math class if seven students are available?

We know we are looking for the number of permutations, since the positions of president and vice-president are not equal.

$$_7P_2 = \frac{7!}{(7-2)!} = \frac{7!}{5!} = \frac{7 \cdot 6 \cdot 5!}{5!} = 7 \cdot 6 = 42$$

It is important to recognize that the number of permutations is a special case of the Counting Principle. Unless we are specifically asked to use the permutation relationship, we use the Counting Principle to solve problems dealing with the number of permutations. For instance, in this example we have seven available students to choose a president from. After we choose a president, we have six available students from which to choose a vice-president.
Hence, using the Counting Principle the ways number of ways we can choose a president and a vice-president = 7.6 = 42.

Combinations

When dealing with the number of **combinations,** the order of element selection is not important. For instance, 2, 3, 4 and 4, 2, 3 are one combination.

The number of combinations represents the number of ways r elements are selected from n elements (in no particular order). We represent the number of combinations as $_nC_r$ and calculate them using the following relationship.

$$_nC_r = \frac{n!}{(n-r)r!}$$

Example: In how many ways can two students be selected from a class of seven students to represent the class?

Since both representatives have the same position, the order is not important and we are dealing with the number of combinations.

$$_nC_r = \frac{7!}{(7-2)!2!} = \frac{7 \cdot 6 \cdot 5!}{5! 2 \cdot 1} = 21$$

Example: In a club there are six women and four men. A committee of two women and one man is to be selected. How many different committees can be selected?

This problem has a sequence of two events. The first event involves selecting two women out of six women and the second event involves selecting one man out of four men. We use the combination relationship to find the number of ways in events 1 and 2 and the Counting Principle to find the number of ways the sequence can happen.

$$\text{\# of Committees} = {_6C_2} \cdot {_4C_1}$$

$$\frac{6!}{(6-2)!2!} \times \frac{4!}{(4-1)!1!}$$

$$= \frac{6 \cdot 5 \cdot 4!}{4! \cdot 2 \cdot 1} \times \frac{4 \cdot 3!}{3! \cdot 1}$$

$$= (15) \times (4) = 60$$

Using tables

Example: The table (below) summarizes the results of a survey of 47 students.

	Black Hair	Blonde Hair	Red Hair	Total
Male	10	8	6	24
Female	6	12	5	23
Total	16	20	11	47

Use the table to answer questions a - c.

a) If we select one student at random, find the probability of selecting a male student.

$$\frac{\text{Number of male students}}{\text{Number of students}} = \frac{24}{47}$$

b) If we select one student at random, find the probability of selecting a female with red hair.

$$\frac{\text{Number of red hair females}}{\text{Number of students}} = \frac{5}{47}$$

c) If we select one student at random, find the probability of selecting a student that does not have red hair.

$$\frac{\text{Red hair students}}{\text{Number of students}} = \frac{11}{47}$$

$$1 - \frac{11}{47} = \frac{36}{47}$$

BASIC SKILLS

Sample Test: Mathematics

1. $\left(\dfrac{-4}{9}\right) + \left(\dfrac{-7}{10}\right) =$

   A. $\dfrac{23}{90}$

   B. $\dfrac{-23}{90}$

   C. $\dfrac{103}{90}$

   D. $\dfrac{-103}{90}$

2. $(5.6) \times (-0.11) =$

   A. -0.616

   B. 0.616

   C. -6.110

   D. 6.110

3. $(3 \times 9)^4 =$

   A. $(3 \times 9)(3 \times 9)(27 \times 27)$

   B. $(3 \times 9) + (3 \times 9)$

   C. (12×36)

   D. $(3 \times 9) + (3 \times 9) + (3 \times 9) + (3 \times 9)$

4. $4\dfrac{2}{9} \times \dfrac{7}{10}$

   A. $4\dfrac{9}{10}$

   B. $\dfrac{266}{90}$

   C. $2\dfrac{43}{45}$

   D. $2\dfrac{6}{20}$

5. $0.74 =$

   A. $\dfrac{74}{100}$

   B. 7.4%

   C. $\dfrac{33}{50}$

   D. $\dfrac{74}{10}$

6. $-9\dfrac{1}{4} \;\square\; -8\dfrac{2}{3}$

   A. $=$

   B. $<$

   C. $>$

   D. $\leq$

BASIC SKILLS

7. 303 is what percent of 600?

    A. 0.505%

    B. 5.05%

    C. 505%

    D. 50.5%

8. An item that sells for $375 is put on sale at $120. What is the percent of decrease?

    A. 25%

    B. 28%

    C. 68%

    D. 34%

9. Two mathematics classes have a total of 410 students. The 8:00 am class has 40 more than the 10:00 am class. How many students are in the 10:00 am class?

    A. 123.3

    B. 370

    C. 185

    D. 330

10. A restaurant employs 465 people. There are 280 waiters and 185 cooks. If 168 waiters and 85 cooks receive pay raises, what percent of the waiters will receive a pay raise?

    A. 36.13%

    B. 60%

    C. 60.22%

    D. 40%

11. For each of the statements below, determine whether $x = \frac{1}{6}$ is a solution.

    i. $6x \leq 4x^2 + 2$
    ii. $10x + 1 = 3(4x - 3)$
    iii. $|x - 1| = x$

    A. i, ii, and iii

    B. i and iii only

    C. i only

    D. iii only

12. A car gets 25.36 miles per gallon. The car has been driven 83,310 miles. What is a reasonable estimate for the number of gallons of gas used?

   A. 2,087 gallons
   B. 3,000 gallons
   C. 1,800 gallons
   D. 164 gallons

13. Identify the missing term in the following harmonic sequence:

   $\dfrac{1}{3}, \dfrac{1}{6}, \dfrac{1}{9}, \dfrac{1}{12}, \dfrac{1}{15}, ?$

   A. $\dfrac{1}{16}$
   B. $\dfrac{1}{17}$
   C. $\dfrac{1}{18}$
   D. 18

14. Round $1\dfrac{13}{16}$ of an inch to the nearest quarter of an inch.

   A. $1\dfrac{1}{4}$ inch
   B. $1\dfrac{5}{8}$ inch
   C. $1\dfrac{3}{4}$ inch
   D. 2 inches

15. The owner of a rectangular piece of land 40 yards in length and 30 yards in width wants to divide it into two parts. She plans to join two opposite corners with a fence as shown in the diagram below. The cost of the fence will be approximately $25 per linear foot. What is the estimated cost for the fence needed by the owner?

   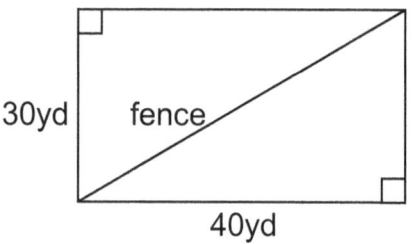

   A. $1,250
   B. $62,500
   C. $5,250
   D. $3,750

16. What unit of measurement could we use to report the distance traveled walking around a track?

   A. degrees
   B. square meters
   C. kilometers
   D. cubic feet

17. What is the area of a square whose side is 13 feet?

   A. 169 feet
   B. 169 square feet
   C. 52 feet
   D. 52 square feet

18. The trunk of a tree has a 2.1 meter radius. What is its circumference?

   A. 2.1π square meters
   B. 4.2π meters
   C. 2.1π meters
   D. 4.2π square meters

19. The figure below shows a running track and the shape of an inscribed rectangle with semicircles at each end.

   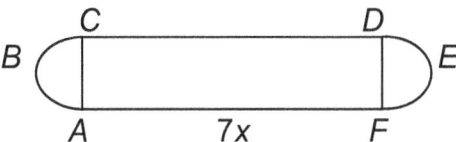

   Calculate the distance around the track.

   A. $6\pi y + 14x$
   B. $3\pi y + 7x$
   C. $6\pi y + 7x$
   D. $3\pi y + 14x$

20. What is the greatest common factor of 16, 28, and 36?

   A. 2
   B. 4
   C. 8
   D. 16

21. Given $f(x) = (x)^3 - 3(x)^2 + 5$, find $x = (-2)$.

   A. 15
   B. -15
   C. 25
   D. -25

22. What type of triangle is $\triangle ABC$?

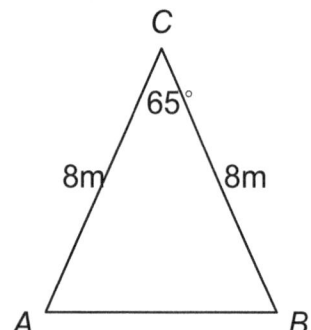

   A. right
   B. equilateral
   C. scalene
   D. isosceles

23. Study figures A, B, C, and D. Select the letter in which all triangles are similar.

   A.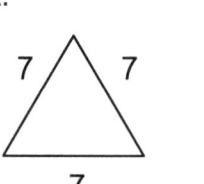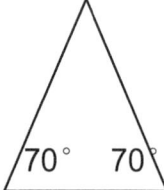

   B.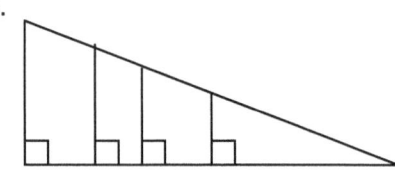

   C.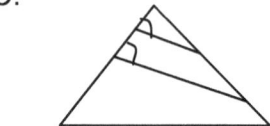

   D.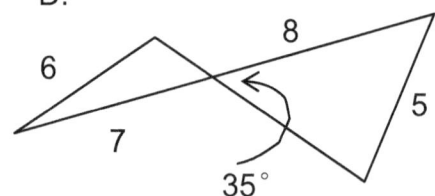

24. Choose the expression that is not equivalent to 5x + 3y + 15z:

   A. 5(x + 3z) + 3y
   B. 3(x + y + 5z)
   C. 3y + 5(x + 3z)
   D. 5x + 3(y + 5z)

25. $\dfrac{7}{9} + \dfrac{1}{3} \div \dfrac{2}{3} =$

   A. $\dfrac{5}{3}$

   B. $\dfrac{3}{2}$

   C. 2

   D. $\dfrac{23}{18}$

26. **Choose the statement that is true for all real numbers.**

   A. $a = 0, b \neq 0$, then $\dfrac{b}{a}$ = undefined.

   B. $^-(a + (^-a)) = 2a$

   C. $2(ab) = ^-(2a)b$

   D. $^-a(b+1) = ab - a$

27. $(^-2.1 \times 10^4)(4.2 \times 10^{-5}) =$

   A. 8.82

   B. -8.82

   C. -0.882

   D. 0.882

28. **Choose the equation that is equivalent to the following:**

   $\dfrac{3x}{5} - 5 = 5x$

   A. $3x - 25 = 25x$

   B. $x - \dfrac{25}{3} = 25x$

   C. $6x - 50 = 75x$

   D. $x + 25 = 25x$

29. If $4x - (3 - x) = 7(x - 3) + 10$, then

   A. $x = 8$

   B. $x = -8$

   C. $x = 4$

   D. $x = -4$

30. **Given the formula $d = rt$, (where d = distance, r = rate, and t = time), calculate the time required for a vehicle to travel 585 miles at a rate of 65 miles per hour.**

   A. 8.5 hours

   B. 6.5 hours

   C. 9.5 hours

   D. 9 hours

BASIC SKILLS

31. The price of gas was $3.27 per gallon. Your tank holds 15 gallons of fuel. You are using two tanks a week. How much will you save weekly if the price of gas goes down to $2.30 per gallon.

    A. $26.00

    B. $29.00

    C. $15.00

    D. $17.00

32. What is the area of this triangle?

    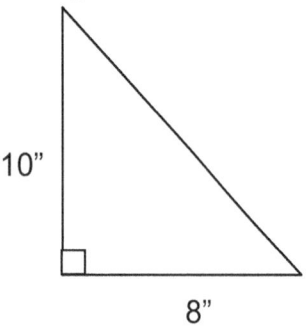

    A. 80 square inches

    B. 20 square inches

    C. 40 square inches

    D. 30 square inches

33. What unit of measurement would describe the spread of a forest fire in a unit time?

    A. 10 square yards per second

    B. 10 yards per minute

    C. 10 feet per hour

    D. 10 cubit feet per hour

34. In a sample of 40 full-time employees at a particular company, 35 were also holding down a part-time job requiring at least 10 hours/week. If this proportion holds for the entire company of 25000 employees, how many full-time employees at this company are actually holding down a part-time job of at least 10 hours per week.

    A. 714

    B. 625

    C. 21,875

    D. 28,571

35. A student organization is interested in determining how strong the support is among registered voters in the United States for the president's education plan. Which of the following procedures would be most appropriate for selecting a statistically unbiased sample?

   A. Having viewers call in to a nationally broadcast talk show and give their opinions.

   B. Survey registered voters selected by blind drawing in the three largest states.

   C. Select regions of the country by blind drawing and then select people from the voters registration list by blind drawing.

   D. Pass out survey forms at the front entrance of schools selected by blind drawing and ask people entering and exiting to fill them in.

36. The following chart shows the yearly average number of international tourists visiting Palm Beach for 1990-1994. How many more international tourists visited Palm Beach in 1994 than in 1991?

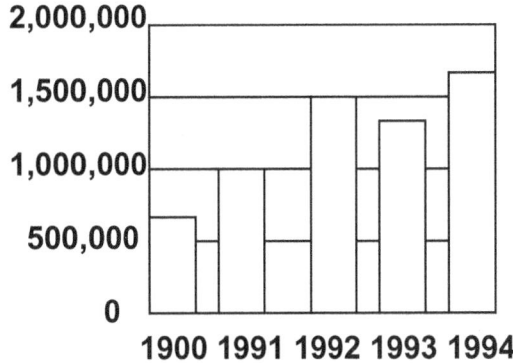

   A. 100,000
   B. 600,000
   C. 1,600,000
   D. 8,000,000

37. What is the mode of the data in the following sample?

   9, 10, 11, 9, 10, 11, 9, 13

   A. 9
   B. 9.5
   C. 10
   D. 11

38. Mary did comparison shopping on her favorite brand of coffee. Over half of the stores priced the coffee at $1.70. Most of the remaining stores priced the coffee at $1.80, except for a few who charged $1.90. Which of the following statements is true about the distribution of prices?

   A. The mean and the mode are the same.
   B. The mean is greater than the mode.
   C. The mean is less than the mode.
   D. The mean is less than the median.

39. Consider the graph of the distribution of the length of time it took individuals to complete an employment form.

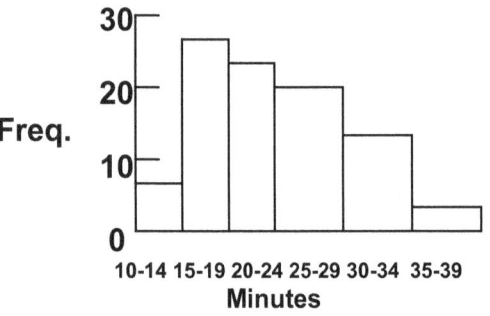

   Approximately how many individuals took less than 15 minutes to complete the employment form?

   A. 35
   B. 28
   C. 7
   D. 4

40. Solve for x.

   $$3x - \frac{2}{3} = \frac{5x}{2} + 2$$

   A. $5\frac{1}{3}$
   B. $\frac{17}{3}$
   C. 2
   D. $\frac{16}{2}$

41. The table below shows the distribution of majors for a group of college students.

Major	Proportion of students
Mathematics	0.32
Photography	0.26
Journalism	0.19
Engineering	0.21
Criminal Law	0.02

   If it is known that a student, chosen at random is not majoring in mathematics or engineering, what is the probability that a student is majoring in journalism?

   A. 0.19
   B. 0.36
   C. 0.40
   D. 0.81

42. For the following statements

   I. All parallelograms are rectangles
   II. Some rhombi are squares

   A. Both statements are correct
   B. Both statements are incorrect
   C. Only II is correct
   D. Only I is correct

43. $\dfrac{2^{10}}{2^5} =$

   A. 2^2
   B. 2^5
   C. 2^{50}
   D. $2^{\frac{1}{2}}$

44. What is the equation that expresses the relationship between x and y in the table below?

x	y
-2	4
-1	1
0	-2
1	-5
2	-8

   A. $y = -x - 2$
   B. $y = -3x - 2$
   C. $y = 3x - 2$
   D. $y = \dfrac{1}{3}x - 1$

45. Set A, B, C, and U are related as shown in the diagram.

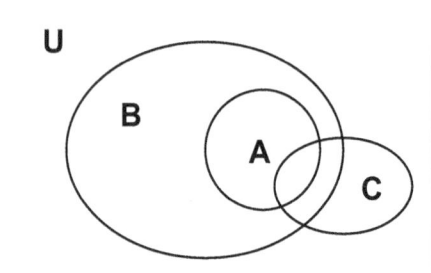

Which of the following is true, assuming not one of the six regions is empty?

A. Any element that is a member of set B is also a member of set A.

B. No element is a member of all three sets A, B, and C.

C. Any element that is a member of set U is also a member of set B.

D. None of the above statements is true.

46. Select the statement that is the negation of the statement, "If the weather is cold, then the soccer game will be played."

A. If the weather is not cold, then the soccer game will be played.

B. The weather is cold and the soccer game was not played.

C. If the soccer game is played, then the weather is not cold.

D. The weather is cold and the soccer game will be played.

47. Select the statement below that is NOT logically equivalent to "If Mary works late, then Bill will prepare lunch."

A. Bill prepares lunch or Mary does not work late.

B. If Bill does not prepare lunch, then Mary did not work late.

C. If Bill prepares lunch, then Mary works late.

D. Mary does not work late or Bill prepares lunch.

48. Select the rule of logical equivalence that directly (in one step) transforms the statement (i) into statement (ii),

   i. Not all the students have books.
   ii. Some students do not have books.

   A. "If p, then q" is equivalent to "if not q, then b."

   B. "Not all are p" is equivalent to "some are not p."

   C. "Not q" is equivalent to "p."

   D. "All are not p" is equivalent to "none are p."

49. Given that:
   i. No athletes are weak.
   ii. All football players are athletes.

   Determine which conclusion can be logically deduced.

   A. Some football players are weak.

   B. All football players are weak.

   C. No football player is weak.

   D. None of the above is true.

50. All of the following arguments have true conclusions, but one of the arguments is not valid. Select the argument that is not valid.

   A. All sea stars are echinoderms and all echinoderms are marine; therefore all sea stars are marine.

   B. All spiders are dangerous. The black widow is dangerous. Therefore, the black widow is a spider.

   C. All crocodiles are amphibians and all amphibians breathe by lungs, gill, or skin; therefore, all crocodiles breathe by lungs, gill, or skin.

   D. All kids have hats and all boys are kids; therefore, all boys have hats.

51. Study the information given below. If a logical conclusion is given, select that conclusion.

Bob eats donuts or he eats yogurt. If Bob eats yogurt, then he is healthy. If Bob is healthy, then he can run the marathon. Bob does not eat yogurt.

A. Bob does not eat donuts.

B. Bob is healthy.

C. If Bob runs the marathon then he eats yogurt.

D. None of the above is warranted.

52. What is the probability of drawing 2 consecutive aces from a standard deck of cards?

A. $\dfrac{3}{51}$

B. $\dfrac{1}{221}$

C. $\dfrac{2}{104}$

D. $\dfrac{2}{52}$

53. A sofa sells for $520. If the retailer makes a 30% profit, what was the wholesale price?

A. $400
B. $676
C. $490
D. $364

54. Corporate salaries are listed for several employees. Which is the best measure of central tendency?

$24,000 $24,000 $26,000
$28,000 $30,000 $120,000

A. Mean
B. median
C. mode
D. no difference

55. Which statement is true about George's budget?

A. George spends the greatest portion of his income on food.
B. George spends twice as much on utilities as he does on his mortgage.
C. George spends twice as much on utilities as he does on food.
D. George spends the same amount on food and utilities as he does on mortgage.

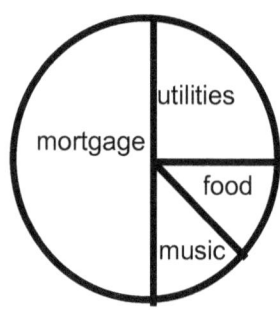

56. Given a drawer with 5 black socks, 3 blue socks, and 2 red socks, what is the probability that you will draw two black socks in two draws in a dark room?

A. 2/9
B. 1/4
C. 17/18
D. 1/18

Answer Key: Mathematics

1.	D		29.	C
2.	A		30.	D
3.	A		31.	B
4.	C		32.	C
5.	A		33.	A
6.	B		34.	C
7.	D		35.	C
8.	C		36.	B
9.	C		37.	A
10.	B		38.	B
11.	C		39.	C
12.	B		40.	A
13.	C		41.	C
14.	C		42.	C
15.	D		43.	B
16.	C		44.	B
17.	B		45.	D
18.	B		46.	B
19.	D		47.	B
20.	B		48.	B
21.	B		49.	C
22.	D		50.	B
23.	B		51.	D
24.	B		52.	B
25.	D		53.	A
26.	A		54.	B
27.	C		55.	C
28.	A		56.	A

TEACHER CERTIFICATION STUDY GUIDE

Rationales for Sample Questions: Mathematics

1. Find the LCD of $\frac{-4}{9}$ and $\frac{-7}{10}$. The LCD is 90, so you get $\frac{-40}{90} + \frac{-63}{90} = \frac{-103}{90}$, which is answer **D**.

2. Simple multiplication. The answer will be negative because a positive times a negative is a negative number. $5.6 \times {}^-0.11 = {}^-0.616$, which is answer **A**.

3. $(3 \times 9)^4 = (3 \times 9)(3 \times 9)(3 \times 9)(3 \times 9)$, which, when solving two of the parentheses, is $(3 \times 9)(3 \times 9)(27 \times 27)$, which is answer **A**.

4. Convert any mixed number to an improper fraction: $\frac{38}{9} \times \frac{7}{10}$. Since no common factors of numerators or denominators exist, multiply the numerators and the denominators by each other $= \frac{266}{90}$. Convert back to a mixed number and reduce $2\frac{86}{90} = 2\frac{43}{45}$. The answer is **C**.

5. $0.74 \rightarrow$ the 4 is in the hundredths place, so the answer is $\frac{74}{100}$, which is **A**.

6. The larger the absolute value of a negative number, the smaller the negative number is. The absolute value of $-9\frac{1}{4}$ is $9\frac{1}{4}$ which is larger than the absolute value of $-8\frac{2}{3}$, which is $8\frac{2}{3}$. Therefore, the relationship should be $-9\frac{1}{4} < -8\frac{2}{3}$, which is answer **B**.

7. Use x for the percent. $600x = 303$. $\frac{600x}{600} = \frac{303}{600} \rightarrow x = 0.505 = 50.5\%$, which is answer **D**.

8. Use $(1 - x)$ as the discount. $375x = 120$.
$375(1-x) = 120 \rightarrow 375 - 375x = 120 \rightarrow 375x = 255 \rightarrow x = 0.68 = 68\%$ which is answer **C**.

9. Let x = # of students in the 8 am class and $x - 40$ = # of students in the 10 am class. $x + (x - 40) = 410 \rightarrow 2x - 40 = 410 \rightarrow 2x = 450 \rightarrow x = 225$. So there are 225 students in the 8 am class, and 225 – 40 = 185 in the 10 am class, which is answer **C**.

10. The total number of waiters is 280 and only 168 of them get a pay raise. Divide the number getting a raise by the total number of waiters to get the percent. $\frac{168}{280} = 0.6 = 60\%$, which is answer **B**.

BASIC SKILLS

TEACHER CERTIFICATION STUDY GUIDE

11. Substitute $x = \dfrac{1}{6}$ into each equation and solve.

i. $6\left(\dfrac{1}{6}\right) \le 4\left(\dfrac{1}{6}\right)^2 + 2 = 1 \le 4\left(\dfrac{1}{36}\right) + 2 \to 1 \le \dfrac{1}{9} + 2 \to 1 \le 2\dfrac{1}{9}$ True.

ii. $10\left(\dfrac{1}{6}\right) + 1 = 3\left(4\left(\dfrac{1}{6}\right) - 3\right) = 2\dfrac{2}{3} = 3\left(\dfrac{2}{3} - 3\right) \to 2\dfrac{2}{3} = \dfrac{6}{3} - 9 \to 2\dfrac{2}{3} = {}^-7$ False.

iii. $\left|\dfrac{1}{6} - 1\right| = \dfrac{1}{6} \to \left|\dfrac{1}{6} - \dfrac{6}{6}\right| = \dfrac{1}{6} \to \left|\dfrac{-5}{6}\right| = \dfrac{1}{6} \to \dfrac{5}{6} = \dfrac{1}{6}$ False.

So, only (i) is true, which is answer **C**.

12. Divide the number of miles by the miles per gallon to determine the approximate number of gallons of gas used.

$\dfrac{83310 \text{ miles}}{25.36 \text{ miles per gallon}} = 3285$ gallons. This is approximately 3000 gallons, which is answer **B**.

13. The difference between the denominators is 3, so the next term in the progression is $\dfrac{1}{18}$, so the answer is **C**.

14. $1\dfrac{13}{16}$ inches is approximately $1\dfrac{12}{16}$, which is also $1\dfrac{3}{4}$, which is the nearest $\dfrac{1}{4}$ of an inch, so the answer is **C**.

15. Find the length of the diagonal by using the Pythagorean theorem. Let x be the length of the diagonal.

$$30^2 + 40^2 = x^2 \to 900 + 1600 = x^2$$
$$2500 = x^2 \to \sqrt{2500} = \sqrt{x^2}$$
$$x = 50 \text{ yards}$$

Convert to feet. $\dfrac{50 \text{ yards}}{x \text{ feet}} = \dfrac{1 \text{ yard}}{3 \text{ feet}} \to 1500$ feet

It cost $25.00 per linear foot, so the cost is (1500 ft)($25) = $3750, which is answer **D**.

16. Degrees measures angles, square meters measures area, cubic feet measure volume, and kilometers measures length. Kilometers is the only reasonable answer, which is **C**.

17. Area = length times width (*lw*).
Length = 13 feet
Width = 13 feet (square, so length and width are the same).
Area = $13 \times 13 = 169$ square feet.
Area is measured in square feet. So the answer is **B**.

BASIC SKILLS

18. Circumference is $2\pi r$, where r is the radius. The circumference is $2\pi 2.1 = 4.2\pi$ meters (not square meters because we are not measuring area), which is answer **B**.

19. The two semicircles of the track create one circle with a diameter 3y. The circumference of a circle is $C = \pi d$ so $C = 3\pi y$. The length of both sides of the track is 7x each side, so the total circumference around the track is $3\pi y + 7x + 7x = 3\pi y + 14x$, which is answer **D**.

20. The smallest number in this set is 16; its factors are 1, 2, 4, 8, and 16. 16 in the largest factor, but it does not divide into 28 or 36. Neither does 8. 4 does factor into both 28 and 36. The answer is **B**.

21. Substitute x = -2.
$$f(-2) = (^-2)^3 - 3 \times (^-2)^2 + 5$$
$$f(-2) = ^-8 - 3(4) + 5$$
$$f(-2) = ^-8 - 12 + 5$$
$$f(-2) = ^-15$$
The answer is **B**.

22. Two of the sides are the same length, so we know the triangle is either equilateral or isosceles. ∡CAB and ∡CBA are equal, because their sides are. Therefore, $180° = 65° - 2x = \frac{115°}{2} = 57.5°$. Because all three angles are not equal, the triangle is isosceles, so the answer is **D**.

23. Choice A is not correct because one triangle is equilateral and the other is isosceles. Choice C is not correct because the two smaller triangles are similar, but the large triangle is not. Choice D is not correct because the lengths and angles are not proportional to each other. Therefore, the correct answer is **B** because all the triangles have the same angles.

24. 5x + 3y + 15z = (5x + 15z) + 3y = 5(x + 3z) + 3y   A. is true
                = 5x + (3y + 15z) = 5x + 3(y + 5z)   D. is true
                = 37 + (5x + 15z) = 37 + 5(x + 3z)   C is true

We can solve all of these using the associative property and then factoring. However, in B 3(x + y + 5z) by distributive property = 3x + 3y + 15z, which does not equal 5x + 37 + 15z. The answer is **B**.

25. First, do the division.
$$\frac{1}{3} \div \frac{2}{3} = \frac{1}{3} \times \frac{3}{2} = \frac{1}{2}$$
Add.
$$\frac{7}{9} + \frac{1}{2} = \frac{14}{18} + \frac{9}{18} = \frac{23}{18}, \text{ which is answer } \mathbf{D}.$$

26. **A** is the correct answer because any number divided by 0 is undefined.

27. First, multiply -2.1 and 4.2 to get -8.82. Then, multiply 10^4 by 10^{-5} to get 10^{-1}. $^-8.82 \times 10^{-1} = ^-0.882$, which is answer **C**.
28. **A** is the correct answer because it is the original equation multiplied by 5. The other choices alter the answer to the original equation.
29. Solve for *x*.
    $$4x - (3 - x) = 7(x - 3) + 10$$
    $$4x - 3 + x = 7x - 21 + 10$$
    $$5x - 3 = 7x - 11$$
    $$5x = 7x - 11 + 3 \quad\quad \text{The answer is } \mathbf{C}.$$
    $$5x - 7x = ^-8$$
    $$^-2x = ^-8$$
    $$x = 4$$
30. We are given $d = 585$ miles and $r = 65$ miles per hour and $d = rt$. Solve for t. $585 = 65t \to t = 9$ hours, which is answer **D**.
31. 15 gallons x 2 tanks = 30 gallons a week
    = 30 gallons x $3.27 = $98.10
    30 gallons x $2.30 = $69.00
    $98.10 - $69.00 = $29.10 is approximately $29.00. The answer is **B**.
32. The area of a triangle is $\frac{1}{2}bh$.
    $\frac{1}{2} \times 8 \times 10 = 40$ square inches. The answer is **C**.
33. The only appropriate answer is one that describes "an area" of forest consumed per unit time. All answers are not units of area measurement except answer **A**.
34. $\frac{35}{40}$ full time employees have a part time job also. Out of 25,000 full time employees, the number that also have a part time job is
    $\frac{35}{40} = \frac{x}{25000} \to 40x = 875000 \to x = 21875$, so 21875 full time employees also have a part time job. The answer is **C**.
35. **C** is the best answer because it is random and it surveys a larger population.
36. The number of tourists in 1991 was 1,000,000 and the number in 1994 was 1,600,000. Subtract to get a difference of 600,000, which is answer **B**.
37. The mode is the number that appears most frequently. 9 appears 3 times, which is more than the other numbers. Therefore the answer is **A**.
38. Over half the stores priced the coffee at $1.70, so this is the mode. The mean is slightly over $1.70 because other stores priced the coffee at over $1.70. Therefore, the answer is **B**.

39. According to the chart, the number of people who took under 15 minutes is 7, which is answer **C**.

40. $3x(6) - \frac{2}{3}(6) = \frac{5x}{2}(6) + 2(6)$ 6 is the LCD of 2 and 3

    $18x - 4 = 15x + 12$

    $18x = 15x + 16$

    $3x = 16$

    $x = \frac{16}{3} = 5\frac{1}{3}$ which is answer **A**.

41. The proportion of students majoring in math or engineering is 0.32 + 0.21 = 0.53. This means that the proportion of students NOT majoring in math or engineering is 1.00 – 0.53 = 0.47. The proportion of students majoring in journalism out of those not majoring in math or engineering is $\frac{0.19}{0.47} = 0.404$, which is answer **C**.

42. I is false because only some parallelograms are rectangles. II is true. So only II is correct, which is answer **C**.

43. The quotient rule of exponents says $\frac{a^m}{a^n} = a^{(m-n)}$ so $\frac{2^{10}}{2^5} = 2^{(10-5)} = 2^5$ which is answer **B**.

44. Solve by plugging the values of x and y into the equations to see if they work. The answer is **B** because it is the only equation for which the values of x and y are correct.

45. Answer A is incorrect because not all members of set B are also in set A. Answer B is incorrect because there are elements that are members of all three sets A, B, and C. Answer C is incorrect because not all members of set U are members of set B. This leaves answer **D**, which states that none of the above choices are true.

46. B
47. B
48. B
49. C
50. B
51. D
52. There are 4 aces in the 52 card deck. P(first ace) = $\frac{4}{52}$. P(second ace) = $\frac{3}{51}$.

    P(first ace and second ace) = P(first ace)xP(second ace)

    $= \frac{4}{52} \times \frac{3}{51} = \frac{1}{221}$. This is answer **B**.

TEACHER CERTIFICATION STUDY GUIDE

53. $400; Let x be the wholesale price, then x + .30x = 520, 1.30x = 520. divide both sides by 1.30. **A**
54. The median provides the best measure of central tendency in this case where the mode is the lowest number and the mean is disproportionately skewed by the outlier $120,000. **B**
55. George spends twice as much on utilities as he does on food. **C**
56. In this example of conditional probability, the probability of drawing a black sock on the first draw is 5/10. It is implied in the problem that there is no replacement, therefore the probability of obtaining a black sock in the second draw is 4/9. Multiply the two probabilities and reduce to lowest terms. **A**

TEACHER CERTIFICATION STUDY GUIDE

DOMAIN II.   **ENGLISH**

COMPETENCY 6.0   CONCEPTUAL AND ORGANIZATIONAL SKILLS

Skill 6.1   Identify logical order in a written passage

The **organization** of written work includes two factors: the order in which writers have chosen to present the different parts of the discussion or argument, and the relationships that they construct between these parts.

Written ideas need to be presented in a **logical order** so that readers can follow the information easily and quickly. There are many different ways in which to order a series of ideas, but they all share one thing in common: to lead readers along desired paths leading to writers' main ideas. *Some* of the ways in which paragraphs may be organized follow:

Sequence of events – In this type of organization, the details are presented in the order in which they have occurred. Paragraphs that describe a process or procedure, give directions, or outline a given period of time (such as a day or a month) are often arranged chronologically.

Statement support – In this type of organization, the main idea is stated, and the rest of the paragraph explains or proves it. This is also referred to as relative importance. There are four ways in which this type of order is organized: most-to-least, least-to-most, most-least-most, and least-most-least.

Comparison-Contrast – In this type of organization, the compare-contrast pattern is used to present the differences or similarities between or among two or more ideas, actions, events, or things. Usually the topic sentence describes the basic relationship between the ideas or items, and the rest of the paragraph explains this relationship.

Classification – in this type of organization, the paragraph presents grouped information about a topic. The topic sentence usually states the general category, and the rest of the sentences show how various elements of the category have (or to what extent they deviate from) a common base.

Cause and Effect – This pattern describes how two or more events are connected. The main sentence usually states the primary cause(s), the primary effect(s), and the general way in which they are connected. The rest of the sentences explain the connection in more detail.

Spatial/Place – In this type of organization, certain descriptions are organized according to the location of items in relation to each other and to a larger context. The orderly arrangement guides readers' eyes as they mentally envision the scene or place being described.

BASIC SKILLS

Even if the sentences that make up a given paragraph or passage are arranged in logical order, the document as a whole can still seem choppy and the various ideas disconnected. **Transitions**, words that signal relationships between ideas, can help improve the flow of a document. Transitions can help achieve a clear and effective presentation of information by establishing connections between sentences, paragraphs, and whole sections of a document. With transitions, each sentence builds on the ideas in the last, and each paragraph has clear links to the preceding one. As a result, readers receive clear directions on how to piece together writers' ideas in a logically coherent flow. By signaling how to organize, interpret, and react to information, transitions allow a writer to effectively and elegantly explain their ideas

Logical Relationship	Transitional Expression
Similarity	also, in the same way, just as ... so too, likewise, similarly
Exception/Contrast	but, however, in spite of, on the one hand ... on the other hand, nevertheless, nonetheless, notwithstanding, in contrast, on the contrary, still, yet
Sequence/Order	first, second, third, ... next, then, finally
Time	after, afterward, at last, before, currently, during, earlier, immediately, later, meanwhile, now, recently, simultaneously, subsequently, then
Example	for example, for instance, namely, specifically, to illustrate
Emphasis	even, indeed, in fact, of course, truly
Place/Position	above, adjacent, below, beyond, here, in front, in back, nearby, there
Cause and Effect	accordingly, consequently, hence, so, therefore, thus
Additional Support or Evidence	additionally, again, also, and, as well, besides, equally important, further, furthermore, in addition, moreover, then
Conclusion/Summary	finally, in a word, in brief, in conclusion, in the end, in the final analysis, on the whole, thus, to conclude, to summarize, in sum, in summary

The following example shows good logical order and transitions

No one really knows how Valentine's Day started. There are several legends, however, which are often told. The first attributes Valentine's Day to a Christian priest who lived in Rome during the third century under the rule of Emperor Claudius. Rome was at war, and apparently Claudius felt that married men didn't fight as well as bachelors. Consequently, Claudius banned marriage for the duration of the war. But Valentinus, the priest, risked his life to secretly marry couples, in violation of Claudius' law. The second legend is even more romantic. In this story, Valentinus is a prisoner having been condemned to death for refusing to worship pagan deities. While in jail, he fell in love with his jailer's daughter who happened to be blind. Daily, he prayed for her sight to return, and miraculously, it did. On February 14, the day that he was condemned to die, he was allowed to write the young woman a note. In this farewell letter, he promised eternal love and signed at the bottom of the page the now famous words, "Your Valentine."

SKILL 6.2 Identify irrelevant sentences

The main idea of a passage may contain a wide variety of supporting information, but it is important that each sentence be related to the main idea. When a sentence contains information that bears little or no connection to the main idea, it is said to be **irrelevant**. It is important to continually assess whether or not a sentence contributes to the overall task of supporting the main idea. When a sentence is deemed irrelevant, it is best to either omit it from the passage or to make it relevant by one of the following strategies:

1. Adding detail – Sometimes a sentence can seem out of place if it does not contain enough information to link it to the topic. Adding specific information can show how the sentence is related to the main idea.

2. Adding an example – This is especially important in passages in which information is being argued, compared, or contrasted. Examples can support the main idea and give the document overall credibility.

3. Using diction effectively – It is important to understand connotation, avoid ambiguity, and steer clear of too much repetition when selecting words.

4. Adding transitions – Transitions are extremely helpful for making sentences relevant because they are specifically designed to connect one idea to another. They can also reduce a paragraph's choppiness.

The following passage has several irrelevant sentences that are highlighted in bold

The New City Planning Committee is proposing a new capitol building to represent the multicultural face of New City. **The current mayor is a Democrat.** The new capitol building will be on 10th Street across from the grocery store and next to the Recreational Center. It will be within walking distance to the subway and bus depot, as the designers want to emphasize the importance of public transportation. Aesthetically, the building will have a contemporary design featuring a brushed-steel exterior and large, floor-to=ceiling windows. **It is important for employees to have a connection with the outside world even when they are in their offices.** Inside the building, the walls will be moveable. This will not only facilitate a multitude of creative floor plans, but it will also create a focus on open communication and smooth flow of information. **It sounds a bit gimmicky to me.** Finally, the capitol will feature a large outdoor courtyard full of lush greenery and serene fountains. **Work will now seem like Club Med to those who work at the New City capitol!**

TEACHER CERTIFICATION STUDY GUIDE

COMPETENCY 7.0   WORD CHOICE SKILLS

SKILL 7.1   Choose the appropriate word or expression in context

Choose the most effective word or phrase within the context suggested by the sentences.

1) The defendant was accused of money from his employer.

   A) stealing
   B) embezzling
   C) robbing

2) O.J. Simpson's angry disposition_____ his ex-wife Nicole.

   A) mortified
   B) intimidated
   C) frightened

3) Many tourists are attracted to Florida because of its_____climate.

   A) friendly
   B) peaceful
   C) balmy

4) The woman was angry because the tomato juice left an_____stain on her brand-new carpet.

   A) unsightly
   B) ugly
   C) unpleasant

5) After disobeying orders, the army private was_____by his superior officer.

   A) degraded
   B) attacked
   C) reprimanded

6) Sharon's critical evaluation of the student's book report left him feeling _____ , which caused him to want to quit school.

   A) surprised
   B) depressed
   C) discouraged

BASIC SKILLS

7) The life-saving medication created by the scientist had a very_____ impact on further developments in the treatment of cancer.

   A) beneficial
   B) fortunate
   C) miraculous

8) Phantom of The Opera is one of Andrew Lloyd Webber's most successful musicals, largely because of its_____themes.

   A) romantic
   B) melodramatic
   C) imaginary

9) The massive Fourth-of-July fireworks display_____the partygoers with lots of colored light and sound.

   A) disgusted
   B) captivated
   C) captured

10) Many of the residents of Grand Forks, North Dakota were forced to _____their homes because of the flood.

    A) escape
    B) evacuate
    C) exit

ANSWERS : 1.A., 2.C., 3.C., 4.A. ,5.C., 6.C., 7.A., 8.A., 9.B., 10.B.

Choose the sentence that expresses the thought most clearly and effectively and is structurally correct in grammar and syntax.

1) A. The movie was three hours in length, featuring interesting characters, and moved at a fast pace.

   B. The movie was three hours long, featured interesting characters, and moved at a fast pace.

   C. Moving at a fast pace, the movie was three hours long and featured interesting characters.

2) A. We were so offended by the waiter's demeanor that we left the restaurant without paying the check.

   B. The waiter's demeanor offended us so much that without paying the check, we left the restaurant.

   C. We left the restaurant without paying the check because we were offended by the waiter's demeanor.

3) A. In today's society, information about our lives is provided to us by computers.

   B. We rely on computers in today's society to provide us information about our lives.

   C. In today's society, we rely on computers to provide us with information about our lives.

4) A. Folding the sides of the tent carefully, Jack made sure to be quiet so none of the other campers would be woken up.

   B. So none of the other campers would be woken up, Jack made sure to be quiet by folding the sides of the tent carefully.

   C. Folding the sides of the tent carefully, so none of the other campers would wake up, Jack made sure to be quiet.

ANSWER KEY

1) B.
2) A.
3) C.
4) A.

Choose the most effective word or phrase within the context suggested by the sentence(s).

1) The six hundred employees of General Electric were_____by the company due to budgetary cutbacks.

   A) released
   B) terminated
   C) downsized

2) The force of the tornado_____the many residents of the town of Russell, Kansas.

   A) intimidated
   B) repulsed
   C) frightened

3) Even though his new car was a lot easier to drive, Fred_____to walk to work every day because he liked the exercise.

   A) needed
   B) preferred
   C) considered

4) June's parents were very upset over the school board's decision to suspend her from Adams High for a week. Before they filed a lawsuit against the board, they_____with a lawyer to help them make a decision.

   A) consulted
   B) debated
   C) conversed

5) The race car driver's_____in handling the automobile was a key factor in his victory.

   A) patience
   B) precision
   C) determination

6) After impressing the judges with her talent and charm, the beauty contestant_____more popularity by singing an aria from "La Boheme."

   A) captured
   B) scored
   C) gained

7) The stained-glass window was_____after a large brick flew through it during the riot.

A) damaged
B) cracked
C) shattered

8) The class didn't know what happened to the professor until it was_____ by the principal why he dropped out of school.

A) informed
B) discovered
C) explained

9) The giant penthouse on the top of the building allows the billionaire industrialist_____the citizens on the street.

A) to view from above
B) the chance to see
C) to glance at

10) Sally's parents_____her to attend the dance after she promised to return by midnight.

A) prohibited
B) permitted
C) asked

ANSWERS: 1) C., 2) C., 3) B., 4) A., 5) B., 6) C., 7) C., 8) C., 9) C., 10) B

Skill 7.2   Recognize commonly confused or misused words or phrases

Students frequently encounter problems with **homonyms**—words that are pronounced the same as another but that have a different meanings; such as mean as a verb, mean as an adjective; and mean as a noun. Mean is also a homograph, a word spelled the same way as another word.

A similar phenomenon that causes trouble is heteronyms (also sometimes called heterophones), words that are spelled the same but that have different pronunciations and meanings (in other words, they are homographs that differ in pronunciation). Technically speaking, they are homographs that are not homophones. For example, the homographs desert (abandon) and desert (arid region) are heteronyms (pronounced differently); but mean (intend) and mean (average) are not.

Another similar occurrence in English is the capitonym, a word that is spelled the same as another but has different meanings when it is capitalized and may or may not have different pronunciations. Example: polish (to make shiny) and Polish (from Poland).

Some of the most troubling homonyms are those that are spelled differently but sound the same. Examples: its (3d person singular neuter pronoun) and it's ("it is"); there, their (3d person plural pronoun) and they're ("they are").

Others: to, too, two;

Some homonyms/homographs are particularly complicated and troubling. Fluke, for instance is a fish, a flatworm, the end parts of an anchor, the fins on a whale's tail, and a stroke of luck.

Common misused words:

Accept is a verb meaning to receive or to tolerate. **Except** is usually a preposition meaning excluding. Except is also a verb meaning to exclude.

Advice is a noun meaning recommendation. **Advise** is a verb meaning to recommend.

Affect is usually a verb meaning to influence. **Effect** is usually a noun meaning result. Effect can also be a verb meaning to bring about.

An **Allusion** is an indirect reference. An **illusion** is a misconception or false impression.

Add is a verb to mean to put together. **Ad** is a noun that is the abbreviation for the word advertisement.

Ain't is a common nonstandard contraction for the contraction aren't.

Allot is a verb meaning to distribute. **A lot** can be an adverb that means often, or to a great degree. It can also mean a large quantity.

Allowed is used here as an adjective that means permitted. **Aloud** is an adverb that means audibly.

Bare is an adjective that means naked or exposed. It can also indicate a minimum. As a noun, **bear** is a large mammal. As a verb, bear means to carry a heavy burden.

Capitol refers to a city, capitol to a building where lawmakers meet. **Capital** also refers to wealth or resources.

A **chord** is a noun that refers to a group of musical notes. **Cord** is a noun meaning rope or a long electrical line.

Compliment is a noun meaning a praising or flattering remark. **Complement** is a noun that means something that completes or makes perfect.

Climactic is derived from climax, the point of greatest intensity in a series or progression of events. **Climatic** is derived from climate; it refers to meteorological conditions.

Discreet is an adjective that means tactful or diplomatic, **discrete** is an adjective that means separate or distinct.

Dye is a noun or verb used to indicate artificially coloring something. **Die** is a verb that means to pass away. Die is also a noun that means a cube-shaped game piece.

Effect is a noun that means outcome. **Affect** is a verb that means to act or produce an effect on.

Elicit is a verb meaning to bring out or to evoke. **Illicit** is an adjective meaning unlawful

Emigrate means to leave one country or region to settle in another. **Immigrate** means to enter another country and reside there.

Gorilla is a noun meaning a large great ape. **Guerrilla** is a member of a band of irregular soldiers.

Horde is a verb that means to accumulate or store up. **Horde** is a large group

Lead is a verb that means to guide or serve as the head of. It is also a noun that is a type of metal.

Medal is a noun that means an award that is strung round the neck. **Meddle** is a verb that means to involve oneself in a matter without right or invitation. **Metal** is an element such as silver or gold. **Mettle** is a noun meaning toughness or guts.

Morning is a noun indicating the time between midnight and midday. **Mourning** is a verb or noun pertaining to the period of grieving after a death.

Past is a noun meaning a time before now (past, present and future). **Passed** is past tense of the verb "to pass."

Piece is a noun meaning portion. **Peace** is a noun meaning the opposite of war.

Peak is a noun meaning the tip or height to reach the highest point. **Peek** is a verb that means to take a brief look. **Pique** is a verb meaning to incite or raise interest.

Principal is a noun meaning the head of a school or an organization or a sum of money. **Principle** is a noun meaning a basic truth or law.

Rite is a noun meaning a special ceremony. **Right** is an adjective meaning correct or direction. **Write** is a verb meaning to compose in writing.

Than is a conjunction used in comparisons; **then** is an adverb denoting time. That pizza is more than I can eat. Tom laughed, and then we recognized him.

Than is used to compare; both words have the letter a in them.

Then tells when; both are spelled the same, except for the first letter.

There is an adverb specifying place; it is also an expletive. Adverb: Sylvia is lying there unconscious. Expletive: There are two plums left. **Their** is a possessive pronoun. **They're** is a contraction of they are. Fred and Jane finally washed their car. They're later than usual today.

To is a preposition; **too** is an adverb; **two** is a number.

Your is a possessive pronoun; **you're** is a contraction of you are.

Strategies to help students conquer these demons: Practice using them in sentences. Context is useful in understanding the difference. Drill is necessary to overcome the misuses.

To effectively teach language, it is necessary to understand that, as human beings acquire language, they realize that words have denotative and connotative meanings. Generally, denotative words point to things, and connotative words deal with mental suggestions that the words convey. The word skunk has a denotative meaning if the speaker can point to the actual animal as he speaks the word and intends the word to identify the animal. Skunk has connotative meaning depending upon the tone of delivery, the socially acceptable attitudes about the animal, and the speaker's personal feelings about the animal.

Problem Phrases

Correct	Incorrect
Supposed to	Suppose to
Used to	Use to
Toward	Towards
Anyway	Anyways
Couldn't care less	Could care less
For all intents and purposes	For all intensive purposes
Come to see me	Come and see me
En route	In route
Regardless	Irregardless
Second, Third	Secondly, Thirdly

Other confusing words

Lie is an intransitive verb meaning to recline or rest on a surface. Its principal parts are lie, lay, lain. **Lay** is a transitive verb meaning to put or place. Its principal parts are lay, laid.

> Birds lay eggs.
> I lie down for bed around 10 PM.

Set is a transitive verb meaning to put or to place. Its principal parts are set, set, set. **Sit** is an intransitive verb meaning to be seated. Its principal parts are sit, sat, sat.

> I set my backpack down near the front door.
> They sat in the park until the sun went down.

Among is a preposition to be used with three or more items. **Between** is to be used with two items.

> Between you and me, I cannot tell the difference among those three Johnson sisters.

As is a subordinating conjunction used to introduce a subordinating clause, **Like** is a preposition and is followed by a noun or a noun phrase.

> As I walked to the lab, I realized that the recent experiment findings were much like those we found last year.

Can is a verb that means to be able. **May** is a verb that means to have permission. They are only interchangeable in cases of possibility.

> I can lift 250 pounds.
> May I go to Alex's house?

Skill 7.3   Recognize diction and tone appropriate to a given audience

Tailoring language for a particular **audience** is an important skill. Writing to be read by a business associate will surely sound different from writing to be read by a younger sibling. Not only are the vocabularies different, but the formality/informality of the discourse will need to be adjusted.

The things to be aware of in determining what the language should be for a particular audience, then, hinges on two things: **word choice** and formality/informality. The most formal language does not use contractions or slang. The most informal language will probably feature a more casual use of common sayings and anecdotes. Formal language will use longer sentences and will not sound like a conversation. The most informal language will use shorter sentences—not necessarily simple sentences—but shorter constructions and may sound like a conversation.

In both formal and informal writing, there exists a **tone**, or the writer's attitude toward the material and/or readers. Tone may be playful, formal, intimate, angry, serious, ironic, outraged, baffled, tender, serene, depressed, etc. The overall tone of a piece of writing is dictated by both the subject matter and the audience. Tone is also related to the actual words which make up the document, as we attach affective meanings to words, their **connotations**. Gaining this conscious control over language makes it possible to use language appropriately in various situations and to evaluate its uses in literature and other forms of communication. By evoking the proper responses from readers/listeners, we can prompt them to take action.

The following questions are an excellent way to assess the audience and tone of a given piece of writing.

1. Who is your audience? (friend, teacher, business person, someone else)
2. How much does this person know about you and/or your topic?
3. What is your purpose? (to prove an argument, to persuade, to amuse, to register a complaint, to ask for a raise, etc)
4. What emotions do you have about the topic? (nervous, happy, confident, angry, sad, numbness, boredom)
5. What emotions do you want to register with your audience? (anger, nervousness, happiness, boredom, interest)
6. What persona do you need to create in order to achieve your purpose?
7. What choice of language is best suited to achieving your purpose with your particular subject? (slang, friendly but respectful, formal)
8. What emotional quality do you want to transmit to achieve your purpose (matter of fact, informative, authoritative, inquisitive, sympathetic, angry), and to what degree do you want to express this tone?

COMPETENCY 8.0   SENTENCE STRUCTURE SKILLS

Skill 8.1   Recognize correct placement of modifiers

Particular phrases that are not placed near the one word they modify often result in misplaced modifiers. Particular phrases that do not relate to the subject being modified result in dangling modifiers.

Error: Weighing the options carefully, a decision was made regarding the punishment of the convicted murderer.

Problem: Who is weighing the options? No one capable of weighing is named in the sentence; thus, the participial phrase *weighing the options carefully* dangles. This problem can be corrected by adding a subject of the sentence capable of doing the action.

Correction: *Weighing the options carefully, the judge made a decision regarding the punishment of the convicted murderer.*

Error: Returning to my favorite watering hole, brought back many fond memories.

Problem: The person who returned is never indicated, and the participle phrase dangles. This problem can be corrected by creating a dependent clause from the modifying phrase.

Correction: *When I returned to my favorite watering hole, many fond memories came back to me.*

Error: One damaged house stood only to remind townspeople of the hurricane.

Problem: The placement of the misplaced modifier *only* suggests that the sole reason the house remained was to serve as a reminder. The faulty modifier creates ambiguity.

Correction: *Only one damaged house stood, reminding townspeople of the hurricane.*

BASIC SKILLS

Error: Recovered from the five-mile hike, the obstacle course was a piece of cake for the Boy Scout troop.

Problem: The obstacle course is not recovered from the five-mile hike, so the modifying phrase must be placed closer to the word, *troop*, that it modifies.

Correction: *The obstacle course was a piece of cake for the Boy Scout troop, which had just recovered from a five-mile hike.*

PRACTICE EXERCISE: MISPLACED AND DANGLING MODIFIERS

Choose the sentence that expresses the thought most clearly and effectively and that has no error in structure.

1) A. Attempting to remove the dog from the well, the paramedic tripped and fell in also.

   B. As the paramedic attempted to remove the dog from the well, he tripped and fell in also.

   C. The paramedic tripped and fell in also attempting to remove the dog from the well.

2) A. To save the wounded child, a powerful explosion ripped through the operating room as the doctors worked.

   B. In the operating room, as the wounded child was being saved, a powerful explosion ripped through.

   C. To save the wounded child, the doctors worked as an explosion ripped through the operating room.

3) A. One hot July morning, a herd of giraffes screamed wildly in the jungle next to the wildlife habitat.

   B. One hot July morning, a herd of giraffes screamed in the jungle wildly next to the wildlife habitat.

   C. One hot July morning, a herd of giraffes screamed in the jungle next to the wildlife habitat, wildly.

4)   A. Looking through the file cabinets in the office, the photographs of the crime scene revealed a new suspect in the investigation.

         B. Looking through the file cabinets in the office, the detective discovered photographs of the crime scene which revealed a new suspect in the investigation.

         C. A new suspect in the investigation was revealed in photographs of the crime scene that were discovered while looking through the file cabinets in the office.

5)   A. In the grand ballroom, the tables and chairs were moved off to the side to make room for the dancers.

         B. To make room for the dancers, the tables and chairs were moved off to the side in the grand ballroom.

         C. To make room for the dancers, we moved the tables and chairs off to the side in the grand ballroom.

TEACHER CERTIFICATION STUDY GUIDE

ANSWER KEY: PRACTICE EXERCISE FOR MISPLACED AND DANGLING MODIFIERS

1) B   Option B corrects the dangling participle *attempting to remove the dog from the well* by creating a dependent clause introducing the main clause. In Option A, the introductory participle phrase *Attempting...well* does not refer to a paramedic, the subject of the main clause. The word also in Option C incorrectly implies that the paramedic was doing something besides trying to remove the dog.

2) C   Option C corrects the dangling modifier *to save the wounded child* by adding the concrete subject doctors worked. Option A infers that an explosion was working to save the wounded child. Option B never tells who was trying to save the wounded child.

3) A   Option A places the adverb *wildly* closest to the verb screamed, which it modifies. Both Options B and C incorrectly place the modifier away from the verb.

4) B   Option B corrects the modifier *looking through the file cabinets in the office* by placing it next to the detective who is doing the looking. Option A sounds as though the photographs were looking; Option C has no one doing the looking.

5) C   Option C corrects the dangling modifier *to make room for the dancers* by adding the concrete subject *we moved the tables and chairs off to the side*. In Option A, the modifier to make room for the dancers has no word to refer to in the sentence. Option B puts the modifier to make room at the beginning of the sentence, but it still has no referent.

BASIC SKILLS

Skill 8.2 Recognize parallelism, including parallel expressions for parallel ideas

Faulty parallelism

Two or more elements stated in a single clause should be expressed with the same (or parallel) structure (e.g., all adjectives, all verb forms, or all nouns).

Error: She needed to be beautiful, successful, and have fame.

Problem: The phrase to be is followed by two different structures: *beautiful* and *successful* are adjectives, and *have fame* is a verb phrase.

Correction: *She needed to be <u>beautiful</u>, <u>successful</u>, and <u>famous</u>.*
    (adjective) (adjective)   (adjective)
OR
She needed <u>beauty</u>, <u>success</u>, and <u>fame</u>.
    (noun)   (noun)   (noun)

Error: I plan either to sell my car during the spring or during the summer.

Problem: Paired conjunctions (also called correlative conjunctions - such as either-or, both-and, neither-nor, not only-but also) need to be followed with similar structures. In the sentence above, *either* is followed by *to sell my car during the spring*, while *or* is followed only by the phrase *during the summer*.

Correction: *I plan to sell my car during either the spring or the summer.*

Error: The President pledged to lower taxes and that he would cut spending to lower the national debt.

Problem: Since the phrase *to lower taxes* follows the verb *pledged*, a similar structure of to is needed with the phrase *cut spending*.

Correction: *The President pledged to lower taxes and to cut spending to lower the national debt.*
OR
The President pledged that he would lower taxes and cut spending to lower the national debt.

TEACHER CERTIFICATION STUDY GUIDE

PRACTICE EXERCISE: PARALLELISM

Choose the sentence that expresses the thought most clearly and effectively, and that has no error in structure.

1. A. Andy found the family tree, researches the Irish descendents, and he was compiling a book for everyone to read.

   B. Andy found the family tree, researched the Irish descendents, and compiled a book for everyone to read.

   C. Andy finds the family tree, researched the Irish descendents, and compiled a book for everyone to read.

2. A. In the last ten years, computer technology has advanced so quickly that workers have had difficulty keeping up with the new equipment and the increased number of functions.

   B. Computer technology has advanced so quickly in the last ten years that workers have had difficulty to keep up with the new equipment and by increasing number of functions.

   C. In the last ten years, computer technology has advanced so quickly that workers have had difficulty keeping up with the new equipment and the number of functions are increasing.

3. A. The Florida State History Museum contains exhibits honoring famous residents, a video presentation about the state's history, an art gallery featuring paintings and sculptures, and they even display a replica of the Florida Statehouse.

   B. The Florida State History Museum contains exhibits honoring famous residents, a video presentation about the state's history, an art gallery featuring paintings and sculptures, and even a replica of the Florida Statehouse.

   C. The Florida State History Museum contains exhibits honoring famous residents, a video presentation about the state's history, an art gallery featuring paintings and sculptures, and there is even a replica of the Florida Statehouse.

4. A. Either the criminal justice students had too much practical experience and limited academic preparation or too much academic preparation and little practical experience.

   B. The criminal justice students either had too much practical experience and limited academic preparation or too much academic preparation and little practical experience.

   C. The criminal justice students either had too much practical experience and limited academic preparation or had too much academic preparation and little practical experience.

5. A. Filmmaking is an arduous process in which the producer hires the cast and crew, chooses locations for filming, supervises the actual production, and guides the editing.

   B. Because it is an arduous process, filmmaking requires the producer to hire a cast and crew and choose locations, supervise the actual production, and guides the editing.

   C. Filmmaking is an arduous process in which the producer hires the cast and crew, chooses locations for filming, supervises the actual production, and guided the editing.

TEACHER CERTIFICATION STUDY GUIDE

ANSWER KEY: PRACTICE EXERCISE FOR PARALLELISM

1. B   Option B uses parallelism by presenting a series of past tense verbs *found, researched*, and *compiled*. Option A interrupts the parallel structure of past tense verbs: *found, researches*, and *he was compiling*. Option C uses present tense verbs and then shifts to past tense: *finds, researched*, and *compiled*.

2. A   Option A uses parallel structure at the end of the sentence: *the new equipment and the increased amount of functions*. Option B creates a faulty structure with *to keep up with the new equipment and by increasing amount of functions*. Option C creates faulty parallelism with *the amount of functions are increasing*.

3. B   Option B uses parallelism by presenting a series of noun phrases acting as objects of the verb contains. Option A interrupts that parallelism by inserting *they even display*, and Option C interrupts the parallelism with the addition of *there is*.

4. C   In the either-or parallel construction, look for a balance on both sides. Option C creates that balanced parallel structure: *either had...or had*. Options A and B do not create the balance. In Option A, the structure is *Either the students...or too much*. In Option B, the structure is *either had...or too much*.

5. A   Option A uses parallelism by presenting a series of verbs with objects: *hires the cast and crew, chooses locations for filming, supervises the actual production, and guides the editing*. The structure of Option B incorrectly suggests that filmmaking chooses locations, supervises the actual production, and guides the editing. Option C interrupts the series of present tense verbs by inserting the participle *guided*, instead of the present tense guides.

BASIC SKILLS

Skill 8.3   **Recognize fragments, comma splices, and run-on sentences**

Fragments occur (1) if word groups standing alone are missing either a subject or a verb, and (2) if word groups containing a subject and verb and standing alone are actually made dependent because of the use of subordinating conjunctions or relative pronouns.

Error: The teacher waiting for the class to complete the assignment.

Problem: This sentence is not complete because an *ing* word alone does not function as a verb. When a helping verb is added (for example, was waiting), it will become a sentence.

Correction: *The teacher was waiting for the class to complete the assignment.*

Error: Until the last toy was removed from the floor.

Problem: Words such as until, because, although, when, and if make a clause dependent and thus incapable of standing alone. An independent clause must be added to make the sentence complete.

Correction: *Until the last toy was removed from the floor, the kids could not go outside to play.*

Error: The city will close the public library. Because of a shortage of funds.

Problem: The problem is the same as above. The dependent clause must be joined to the independent clause.

Correction: *The city will close the public library because of a shortage of funds.*

Error: Anyone planning to go on the trip should bring the necessary items. Such as a backpack, boots, a canteen, and bug spray.

Problem: The second word group is a phrase and cannot stand alone because there is neither a subject nor a verb. The fragment can be corrected by adding the phrase to the sentence.

Correction: *Anyone planning to go on the trip should bring the necessary items, such as a backpack, boots, a canteen, and bug spray.*

PRACTICE EXERCISE: FRAGMENTS

Choose the option that corrects the underlined portion(s) of the sentence. If no error exists, choose "No change is necessary."

1) Despite the lack of funds in the <u>budget it</u> was necessary to rebuild the roads that were damaged from the recent floods.

   A) budget: it
   B) budget, it
   C) budget; it
   D) No change is necessary

2) After determining that the fire was caused by faulty <u>wiring, the</u> building inspector said the construction company should be fined.

   A) wiring. The
   B) wiring the
   C) wiring; the
   D) No change is necessary

3) Many years after buying a grand <u>piano Henry</u> decided he'd rather play the violin instead.

   A) piano: Henry
   B) piano, Henry
   C) piano; Henry
   D) No change is necessary

4) Computers are being used more and more <u>frequently. because</u> of their capacity to store information.

   A) frequently because
   B) frequently, because
   C) frequently; because
   D) No change is necessary

5) Doug washed the floors <u>every day. to</u> keep them clean for the guests.

   A) every day to
   B) every day,
   C) every day;
   D) No change is necessary.

TEACHER CERTIFICATION STUDY GUIDE

ANSWER KEY: PRACTICE EXERCISE FOR FRAGMENTS

1. B   The clause that begins with *despite* is independent and must be separated with the clause that follows by a comma. Option A is incorrect because a colon is used to set off a list or to emphasize what follows. In Option B, a comma incorrectly suggests that the two clauses are dependent.

2. D   In the test item, a comma correctly separates the dependent clause *After...wiring* at the beginning of the sentence from the independent clause that follows. Option A incorrectly breaks the two clauses into separate sentences, while Options B omits the comma, and Option C incorrectly suggests that the phrase is an independent clause.

3. B   The *phrase Henry decided...instead* must be joined to the independent clause. Option A incorrectly puts a colon before *Henry decided*, and Option C incorrectly separates the phrase as if it were an independent clause.

4. A   The second clause *because...information* is dependent and must be joined to the first independent clause. Option B is incorrect because as the dependent clause comes at the end of the sentence, rather than at the beginning, a comma is not necessary. In Option C, a semi-colon incorrectly suggests that the two clauses are independent.

5. A   The second clause *to keep...guests* is dependent and must be joined to the first independent clause. Option B is incorrect because as the dependent clause comes at the end of the sentence, rather than at the beginning, a comma is not necessary. In Option C, a semi-colon incorrectly suggests that the two clauses are independent.

Comma splices appear when two sentences are joined by only a comma. **Fused sentences** appear when two sentences are run together with no punctuation at all.

Error: Dr. Sanders is a brilliant scientist, his research on genetic disorders won him a Nobel Prize.

Problem: A comma alone cannot join two independent clauses (complete sentences). The two clauses can be joined by a semi-colon, or they can be separated by a period.

Correction: *Dr. Sanders is a brilliant scientist; his research on genetic disorders won him a Nobel Prize.*
OR
Dr. Sanders is a brilliant scientist. His research on genetic disorders won him a Nobel Prize.

Error: Florida is noted for its beaches they are long, sandy, and beautiful.

Problem: The first sentence ends with the word beaches, and the second sentence cannot be joined with the first. The fused sentence error can be corrected in several ways: (1) one clause may be made dependent on another with a subordinating conjunction or a relative pronoun; (2) a semi-colon may be used to combine two equally important ideas; (3) the two independent clauses may be separated by a period.

Correction: *Florida is noted for its beaches, which are long, sandy, and beautiful.*
OR
Florida is noted for its beaches; they are long, sandy, and beautiful.
OR
Florida is noted for its beaches. They are long, sandy, and beautiful.

Error: The number of hotels has increased, however, the number of visitors has grown also.

Problem: The first sentence ends with the word 'increased,' and a comma is not strong enough to connect it to the second sentence. The adverbial transition however does not function the same way as a coordinating conjunction and cannot be used with commas to link two sentences. Several different corrections are available.

Correction: *The number of hotels has increased; however, the number of visitors has grown also.*
[Two separate but closely related sentences are created with the use of the semicolon.]

OR

The number of hotels has increased. However, the number of visitors has grown also.
[Two separate sentences are created.]

OR

Although the number of hotels have increased, the number of visitors has grown also.
[One idea is made subordinate to the other and separated with a comma.]

OR

The number of hotels have increased, but the number of visitors has grown also.

[The comma before the coordinating conjunction *but* is appropriate. The adverbial transition 'however' does not function the same way as the coordinating conjunction but does.]

TEACHER CERTIFICATION STUDY GUIDE

PRACTICE EXERCISE: FUSED SENTENCES AND COMMA SPLICES

Choose the option that corrects an error in the underlined portion(s). If no error exists, choose "No change is necessary".

1) Scientists are excited at the ability to clone a <u>sheep; however,</u> it is not yet known if the same can be done to humans.

    A) sheep, however,
    B) sheep. However,
    C) sheep, however;
    D) No change is necessary

2) Because of the rising cost of college <u>tuition the</u> federal government now offers special financial assistance, <u>such as loans,</u> to students.

    A) tuition, the
    B) tuition; the
    C) such as loans
    D) No change is necessary

3) As the number of homeless people continue to <u>rise, the major cities</u> like <u>New York and Chicago,</u> are now investing millions of dollars in low-income housing.

    A) rise. The major cities
    B) rise; the major cities
    C) New York and Chicago
    D) No change is necessary

4) Unlike in <u>the 1950's, most</u> households find the husband and wife working full-time to make <u>ends meet in many</u> different career fields.

    A) the 1950's; most
    B) the 1950's most
    C) ends meet, in many
    D) No change is necessary

BASIC SKILLS

ANSWER KEY : PRACTICE EXERCISE FOR COMMA SPLICES AND FUSED SENTENCES

1) B   Option B correctly separates two independent clauses. The comma in Option A after the word sheep creates a run-on sentence. The semi-colon in Option C does not separate the two clauses but occurs at an inappropriate point.

2) A   The comma in Option A correctly separates the independent clause and the dependent clause. The semi-colon in Option B is incorrect because one of the clauses is independent. Option C requires a comma to prevent a run-on sentence.

3) C   Option C is correct because a comma creates a run-on. Option A is incorrect because the first clause is dependent. The semi-colon in Option B incorrectly divides the dependent clause from the independent clause.

4) D   Option D correctly separates the two clauses with a comma. Option A incorrectly uses a semi-colon to divide the clauses. The lack of a comma in Option B creates a run-on sentence. Option C puts a comma in an inappropriate place.

COMPETENCY 9.0 GRAMMAR, SPELLING, CAPITALIZATION, AND PUNCTUATION SKILLS

Skill 9.1 Identify standard verb forms

Past tense and past participles
Both regular and irregular verbs must appear in their standard forms for each tense. Note: the *ed* or *d* ending is added to regular verbs in the past tense and for past participles.

Infinitive	Past Tense	Past Participle
Bake	Baked	Baked

Irregular Verb Forms

Infinitive	Past Tense	Past Participle
Be	Was, were	Been
Become	Became	Become
Break	Broke	Broken
Bring	Brought	Brought
Choose	Chose	Chosen
Come	Came	Come
Do	Did	Done
Draw	Drew	Drawn
Eat	Ate	Eaten
Fall	Fell	Fallen
Forget	Forgot	Forgotten
Freeze	Froze	Frozen
Give	Gave	Given
Go	Went	Gone
Grow	Grew	Grown
Have/has	Had	Had
Hide	Hid	Hidden
Know	Knew	Known
Lay	Laid	Laid
Lie	Lay	Lain
Ride	Rode	Ridden
Rise	Rose	Risen
Run	Ran	Run
See	Saw	Seen
Steal	Stole	Stolen
Take	Took	Taken
Tell	Told	Told
Throw	Threw	Thrown
Wear	Wore	Worn
Write	Wrote	Written

Error: She should have went to her doctor's appointment at the scheduled time.

Problem: The past participle of the verb *to go* is *gone*. *Went* expresses the simple past tense.

Correction: *She should have gone to her doctor's appointment at the scheduled time.*

Error: My train is suppose to arrive before two o'clock.

Problem: The verb following *train* is a present tense passive construction which requires the present tense verb *to be* and the past participle.

Correction: *My train is supposed to arrive before two o'clock.*

Error: Linda should of known that the car wouldn't start after leaving it out in the cold all night.

Problem: *Should of* is a nonstandard expression. *Of is* not a verb.

Correction: *Linda should have known that the car wouldn't start after leaving it out in the cold all night.*

PRACTICE EXERCISE: STANDARD VERB FORMS

Choose the option that corrects an error in the underlined portion(s). If no error exists, choose "No change is necessary."

1) My professor had knew all along that we would pass his course.

   A. know
   B. had known
   C. knowing
   D. No change is necessary

2) Kevin was asked to erase the vulgar words he had wrote.

   A. writes
   B. has write
   C. had written
   D. No change is necessary

3) Melanie had forget to tell her parents that she left the cat in the closet.

   A. had forgotten
   B. forgot
   C. forget
   D. No change is necessary

4) Craig always leave the house a mess when his parents aren't there.

   A. left
   B. leaves
   C. leaving
   D. No change is necessary

5) The store manager accused Kathy of having stole more than five hundred dollars from the safe.

   A. has stolen
   B. having stolen
   C. stole
   D. No change is necessary

TEACHER CERTIFICATION STUDY GUIDE

ANSWER KEY : PRACTICE EXERCISE FOR STANDARD VERB FORMS

1. B — Option B is correct because the past participle needs the helping verb *had*. Option A is incorrect because *it* is in the infinitive tense. Option C incorrectly uses the present participle.

2. C — Option C is correct because the past participle follows the helping verb *had*. Option A uses the verb in the present tense. Option B is an incorrect use of the verb.

3. A — Option A is correct because the past participle uses the helping verb *had*. Option B uses the wrong form of the verb. Option C uses the wrong form of the verb.

4. B — Option B correctly uses the past tense of the verb. Option A uses the verb in an incorrect way. Option C uses the verb without a helping verb like *is*.

5. B — Option B is correct because it is the past participle. Option A and C use the verb incorrectly.

Skill 9.2 Identify inappropriate shifts in verb tense

Unless a change in time is required, verb tenses must refer to the same time period consistently.

Error: Despite the increased amount of students in the school this year, overall attendance is higher last year at the sporting events.

Problem: The verb *is* represents an inconsistent shift to the present tense when the action refers to a past occurrence.

Correction: *Despite the increased amount of students in the school this year, overall attendance was higher last year at sporting events.*

Error: My friend Lou, who just competed in the marathon, ran since he was twelve years old.

Problem: Because Lou continues to run, the present perfect tense is needed.

Correction: *My friend Lou, who just competed in the marathon, has ran since he was twelve years old.*

Error: The Mayor congratulated Wallace Mangham, who renovates the city hall last year.

Problem: Although the speaker is talking in the present, the action of renovating the city hall was in the past.

Correction: *The Mayor congratulated Wallace Mangham, who renovated the city hall last year.*

PRACTICE EXERCISE: SHIFTS IN TENSE

Choose the option that corrects an error in the underlined portion(s).
If no error exists, choose "No change is necessary".

1) After we <u>washed</u> the fruit that had <u>growing</u> in the garden, we knew there <u>was</u> a store that would buy them.

   A) washing
   B) grown
   C) is
   D) No change is necessary.

2) The tourists <u>used</u> to visit the Atlantic City boardwalk whenever they <u>vacationed</u> during the summer. Unfortunately, their numbers have <u>diminished</u> every year.

   A) use
   B) vacation
   C) diminish
   D) No change is necessary.

3) When the temperature <u>drops</u> to below thirty-two degrees Fahrenheit, the water on the lake <u>freezes</u>, which <u>allowed</u> children to skate across it.

   A) dropped
   B) froze
   C) allows
   D) No change is necessary.

4) The artists were <u>hired</u> to <u>create</u> a monument that would pay tribute to the men who were <u>killed</u> in World War Two.

   A) hiring
   B) created
   C) killing
   D) No change is necessary.

5) Emergency medical personnel rushed to the scene of the shooting, where many injured people <u>waiting</u> for treatment.

   A) wait
   B) waited
   C) waits
   D) No change is necessary.

TEACHER CERTIFICATION STUDY GUIDE

ANSWER KEY : PRACTICE EXERCISE FOR SHIFTS IN TENSE

1) B   The past participle *grown* is needed instead of *growing* which is the progressive tense. Option A is incorrect because the past participle *washed* takes the *ed*. Option C incorrectly replaces the past participle *was* with the present tense *is*.

2) D   Option A is incorrect because *use* is the present tense. Option B incorrectly uses the noun *vacation*. Option C incorrectly uses the present tense *diminish* instead of the past tense *diminished*.

3) C   The present tense *allows* is necessary in the context of the sentence. Option A is incorrect because *dropped* is a past participle. Option B is incorrect because *froze* is also a past participle.

4) D   In Option A is incorrect because *hiring* is the present tense. In Option B is incorrect because *created* is a past participle. In Option C, *killing*, doesn't fit into the context of the sentence.

5) B   In Option B, *waited*, corresponds with the past tense *rushed*. In Option A, *wait*, is incorrect because it is present tense. In Option C, *waits*, is incorrect because the noun *people* is plural and requires the singular form of the verb.

TEACHER CERTIFICATION STUDY GUIDE

Skill 9.3   **Identify agreement between subject and verb**

A verb must correspond in the singular or plural form with the simple subject; it is not affected by any interfering elements. Note: A simple subject is never found in a prepositional phrase (a phrase beginning with a word such as of, by, over, through, until).

Present Tense Verb Form

	Singular	Plural
1st person (talking about oneself)	I do	We do
2nd person (talking to another)	You do	You do
3rd person (talking about someone or something)	He She does It	They do

Error: Sally, as well as her sister, plan to go into nursing.

Problem: The subject in the sentence is *Sally* alone, not the word *sister*. Therefore, the verb must be singular.

Correction: *Sally, as well as her sister, plans to go into nursing.*

Error: There has been many car accidents lately on that street.

Problem: The subject accidents in this sentence is plural; the verb must be plural also --even though it comes before the subject.

Correction: *There have been many car accidents lately on that street.*

Error: Everyone of us have a reason to attend the school musical.

Problem: The simple subject is the word *everyone*, not the *us* in the prepositional phrase. Therefore, the verb must be singular also.

Correction: *Everyone of us has a reason to attend the school musical.*

Error: Either the police captain or his officers is going to the convention.

Problem: In either/or and neither/nor constructions, the verb agrees with the subject closer to it.

Correction: *Either the police captain or his officers are going to the convention.*

BASIC SKILLS

TEACHER CERTIFICATION STUDY GUIDE

PRACTICE EXERCISE: SUBJECT-VERB AGREEMENT

Choose the option that corrects an error in the underlined portion(s).
If no error exists, choose "No change is necessary."

1) Every year ,the store <u>stays</u> open late, when shoppers desperately <u>try</u> to purchase Christmas presents as they <u>prepare</u> for the holiday.

   A. stay
   B. tries
   C. prepared
   D. No change is necessary.

2) Paul McCartney, together with George Harrison and Ringo Starr, <u>sing</u> classic Beatles songs on a special greatest-hits CD.

   A. singing
   B. sings
   C. sung
   D. No change is necessary.

3) My friend's cocker spaniel, while <u>chasing</u> cats across the street, always <u>manages</u> to <u>knock</u> over the trash cans.

   A. chased
   B. manage
   C. knocks
   D. No change is necessary.

4) Some of the ice on the driveway <u>have melted.</u>

   A. having melted
   B. has melted
   C. has melt.
   D. No change is necessary.

5) Neither the criminal forensics expert nor the DNA blood evidence <u>provided</u> enough support for that verdict.

   A. provides
   B. were providing
   C. are providing
   D. No change is necessary.

BASIC SKILLS

ANSWER KEY: PRACTICE EXERCISE FOR SUBJECT-VERB AGREEMENT

1) D — Option D is correct because *store* is third person singular and requires the third person singular verbs *stays*. Option B is incorrect because the plural noun *shoppers* requires a plural verb *try*. In Option C, there is no reason to shift to the past tense *prepared*.

2) B — Option B is correct because the subject, *Paul McCartney*, is singular and requires the singular verb *sings*. Option A is incorrect because the present participle *singing* does not stand alone as a verb. Option C is incorrect because the past participle *sung* alone cannot function as the verb in this sentence.

3) D — Option D is the correct answer because the subject *cocker spaniel* is singular and requires the singular verb *manages*. Options A, B, and C do not work structurally with the sentence.

4) B — The subject of the sentence is *some*, which requires a third person singular verb, *has melted*. Option A incorrectly uses the present participle *having*, which does not act as a helping verb. Option C does not work structurally with the sentence.

5) A — In Option A, the singular subject *evidence* is closer to the verb and thus requires the singular in the neither/nor construction. Both Options B and C are plural forms with the helping verb and the present participle.

Skill 9.4 Identify agreements between pronoun and antecedent

A pronoun must correspond to its antecedent in number (singular or plural), person (first, second or third person) and gender (male, female or neutral). A pronoun must refer clearly to a single word, not to a complete idea.

A **pronoun shift** is a grammatical error in which the author starts a sentence, paragraph, or section of a paper using one particular type of pronoun and then suddenly shifts to another. This often confuses the reader.

Error: A teacher should treat all their students fairly.

Problem: Since *A teacher* is singular, the pronoun referring to it must also be singular. Otherwise, the noun has to be made plural.

Correction: *Teachers should treat all their students fairly.*

Error: When an actor is rehearsing for a play, it often helps if you can memorize the lines in advance.

Problem: *Actor* is a third-person word; that is, the writer is talking about the subject. The pronoun *you* is in the second person, which means the writer is talking to the subject.

Correction: *When actors are rehearsing for plays, it helps if they can memorize the lines in advance.*

Error: The workers in the factory were upset when his or her paychecks didn't arrive on time.

Problem: *Workers* is a plural form, while *his or her* refers to one person.

Correction: *The workers in the factory were upset when their paychecks didn't arrive on time.*

Error: The charity auction was highly successful, which pleased everyone.

Problem: In this sentence the pronoun *which* refers to the idea of the auction's success. In fact, *which* has no antecedent in the sentence; the word success is not stated.

Correction: *Everyone was pleased at the success of the auction.*

BASIC SKILLS

Error: Lana told Melanie that she would like aerobics.
Problem: The person that she refers to is unclear; it could be either Lana or Melanie.

Correction: *Lana said that Melanie would like aerobics.*

OR

Lana told Melanie that she, Melanie, would like aerobics.

Error: I dislike accounting, even though my brother is one.

Problem: A person's occupation is not the same as a field, and the pronoun *one* is thus incorrect. Note that the word *accountant* is not used in the sentence, so *one* has no antecedent.

Correction: *I dislike accounting, even though my brother is an accountant.*

TEACHER CERTIFICATION STUDY GUIDE

PRACTICE EXERCISE: PRONOUN/ANTECEDENT AGREEMENT

Choose the option that corrects an error in the underlined portion(s).
If no error exists, choose "No change is necessary."

1) <u>You</u> can get to Martha's Vineyard by driving from Boston to Woods Hole. Once there, you can travel over on a ship, but <u>you</u> may find traveling by <u>airplane</u> to be an exciting experience.

   A. They
   B. visitors
   C. it
   D. No change is necessary.

2) Both the city leader and the <u>journalist</u> are worried about the new interstate; <u>she fears</u> <u>the new roadway</u> will destroy precious farmland.

   A. journalist herself
   B. they fear
   C. it
   D. No change is necessary.

3) When <u>hunters</u> are looking for deer in <u>the woods, you</u> must remain quiet for long periods of time.

   A. they
   B. it
   C. we
   D. No change is necessary.

4) Florida's strong economy is based on the importance of the citrus industry. <u>Producing</u> orange juice for most of the country.

   A. They produce
   B. Who produce
   C. Farmers there produce
   D. No change is necessary.

5) Dr. Kennedy told Paul Elliot, <u>his</u> assistant, that <u>he</u> would have to finish grading the tests before going home, no matter how long <u>it</u> took.

   A. their
   B. he, Paul
   C. they
   D. No change is necessary.

BASIC SKILLS

TEACHER CERTIFICATION STUDY GUIDE

ANSWER KEY: PRACTICE EXERCISE FOR PRONOUN AGREEMENT

1) D — Pronouns must be consistent. As *you* is used throughout the sentence, the shift to *visitors* is incorrect. Option A, *They*, is vague and unclear. Option C, *it*, is also unclear.

2) B — The plural pronoun *they* is necessary to agree with the two nouns *leader* and *journalist*. There is no need for the reflexive pronoun *herself* in Option A. Option C, *it*, is vague.

3) A — The shift to *you* is unnecessary. The plural pronoun *they* is necessary to agree with the noun *hunters*. The word *we* in Option C is vague; the reader does not know who the word *we* might refer to. Option B, *it*, has no antecedent.

4) C — The noun *farmers* is needed for clarification because *producing* is vague. Option A is incorrect because *they produce* is vague. Option B is incorrect because *who* has no antecedent and creates a fragment.

5) B — The repetition of the name *Paul* is necessary to clarify who the pronoun *he* is referring to. (It could be Dr. Kennedy.) Option A is incorrect because the singular pronoun *his* is needed, not the plural pronoun *their*. Option C is incorrect because the pronoun *it* refers to the plural noun *tests*.

Skill 9.5   Identify inappropriate pronoun shifts

See Skill 9.4

Skill 9.6 Identify clear pronoun references

Rules for clearly identifying pronoun reference

Make sure that the antecedent reference is clear and cannot refer to something else

A "distant relative" is a relative pronoun or a relative clause that has been placed too far away from the antecedent to which it refers. it is a common error to place a verb between the relative pronoun and its antecedent.

Error: Return the books to the library that are overdue.
Problem: The relative clause "that are overdue" refers to the "books" and should be placed immediately after the antecedent.
Correction: Return the books that are overdue to the library.

or

Return the overdue books to the library.

A pronoun should not refer to adjectives or possessive nouns

Adjectives, nouns or possessive pronouns should not be used as antecedents. This will create ambiguity in sentences.

Error: In Todd's letter he told his mom he'd broken the priceless vase.
Problem: In this sentence the pronoun "he" seems to refer to the noun phrase "Todd's letter" though it was probably meant to refer to the possessive noun "Todd's."
Correction: In his letter, Todd told his mom that he had broken the priceless vase.

A pronoun should not refer to an implied idea

A pronoun must refer to a specific antecedent rather than an implied antecedent. When an antecedent is not stated specifically, the reader has to guess or assume the meaning of a sentence. Pronouns that do not have antecedents are called expletives. "It" and "there" are the most common expletives, though other pronouns can also become expletives as well. In informal conversation, expletives allow for casual presentation of ideas without supporting evidence. However, in more formal writing, it is best to be more precise.

Error: She said that it is important to floss every day.
Problem: The pronoun "it" refers to an implied idea.
Correction: She said that flossing every day is important.

Error: They returned the book because there were missing pages.
Problem: The pronouns "they" and "there" do not refer to the antecedent.
Correction: The customer returned the book with missing pages.

Using Who, That and Which

Who, whom and **whose** refer to human beings and can either introduce essential or nonessential clauses. **That** refers to things other than humans and is used to introduce essential clauses. **Which** refers to things other than humans and is used to introduce nonessential clauses.

Error: The doctor that performed the surgery said the man would be fully recovered.
Problem: Since the relative pronoun is referring to a human, who should be used.
Correction: The doctor who performed the surgery said the man would be fully recovered.

Error: That ice cream cone that you just ate looked really delicious.
Problem: That has already been used so you must use *which* to introduce the next clause, whether it is essential or nonessential.
Correction: That ice cream cone, which you just ate, looked really delicious.

Skill 9.7   Identify proper case forms

Pronouns, unlike nouns, change case forms. Pronouns must be in the subjective, objective, or possessive form according to their function in the sentence.

Personal Pronouns

	Subjective (Nominative)		Possessive		Objective	
	Singular	Plural	Singular	Plural	Singular	Plural
1st person	I	We	My	Our	Me	Us
2nd person	You	You	Your	Your	You	You
3rd person	He She It	They	His Her Its	Their	Him Her It	them

Relative Pronouns
Who   Subjective/Nominative
Whom   Objective
Whose   Possessive

Error: Tom and me have reserved seats for next week's baseball game.

Problem: The pronoun *me* is the subject of the verb *have reserved* and should be in the subjective form.

Correction: *Tom and I have reserved seats for next week's baseball game.*

Error: Mr. Green showed all of we students how to make paper hats.

Problem: The pronoun *we* is the object of the preposition *of*. It should be in the objective form, us.

Correction*: Mr. Green showed all of us students how to make paper hats.*

Error: Who's coat is this?

Problem: The interrogative possessive pronoun is whose; *who's* is the contraction for who is.

Correction: *Whose coat is this?*

Error: The voters will choose the candidate whom has the best qualifications for the job.

Problem: The case of the relative pronoun *who* or *whom* is determined by the pronoun's function in the clause in which it appears. The word *who* is in the subjective case, and *whom* is in the objective. Analyze how the pronoun is being used within the sentence.

Correction: *The voters will choose the candidate who has the best qualifications for the job.*

PRACTICE EXERCISE: PRONOUN CASE

Choose the option that corrects an error in the underlined portion(s).
If no error exists, choose "No change is necessary".

1) Even though Sheila and <u>he</u> had planned to be alone at the diner, <u>they</u> were joined by three friends of <u>their's</u> instead.

   A) him
   B) him and her
   C) theirs
   D) No change is necessary.

2) Uncle Walter promised to give his car to <u>whomever</u> will guarantee to drive it safely.

   A) whom
   B) whoever
   C) them
   D) No change is necessary.

3) Eddie and <u>him</u> gently laid <u>the body</u> on the ground next to <u>the sign</u>.

   A) he
   B) them
   C) it
   D) No change is necessary.

4) Mary, <u>who</u> is competing in the chess tournament, is a better player than <u>me</u>.

   A) whose
   B) whom
   C) I
   D) No change is necessary.

5) <u>We, ourselves,</u> have decided not to buy property in that development; however, our friends have already bought <u>themselves</u> some land.

   A) We, ourself,
   B) their selves
   C) their self
   D) No change is necessary.

BASIC SKILLS

TEACHER CERTIFICATION STUDY GUIDE

ANSWER KEY : PRACTICE EXERCISE FOR PRONOUN CASE

1) C — The possessive pronoun *theirs* doesn't need an apostrophe. Option A is incorrect because the subjective pronoun *he* is needed in this sentence. Option B is incorrect because the subjective pronoun *they*, not the objective pronouns *him* and *her*, is needed.

2) B — The subjective case *whoever*--not the objective case *whomever*--is the subject of the relative clause *whoever will guarantee to drive it safely*. Option A is incorrect because *whom* is an objective pronoun. Option C is incorrect because *car* is singular and takes the pronoun *it*.

3) A — The subjective pronoun *he* is needed as the subject of the verb *laid*. Option B is incorrect because *them* is vague; the noun *body* is needed to clarify *it*. Option C is incorrect because *it* is vague, and the noun *sign* is necessary for clarification.

4) C — The nominative, or subject, pronoun *I* is needed because the comparison is understood. Option A incorrectly uses the possessive *whose*. Option B is incorrect because the subjective pronoun *who*, and not the objective *whom*, is needed.

5) B — The reflexive pronoun *themselves* refers to the plural *friends*. Option A is incorrect because the plural *we* requires the reflexive *ourselves*. Option C is incorrect because the possessive pronoun *their* is never joined with either *self* or *selves*.

Skill 9.8 Identify the correct use of adjectives and adverbs

Adjectives are words that modify or describe nouns or pronouns. Adjectives usually precede the words they modify, but not always; for example, an adjective occurs after a linking verb.

Adverbs are words that modify verbs, adjectives, or other adverbs. They cannot modify nouns. Adverbs answer such questions as how, why, when, where, how much, or how often something is done. Many adverbs are formed by adding *ly*.

Error: The birthday cake tasted sweetly.

Problem: *Tasted* is a linking verb; the modifier that follows should be an adjective, not an adverb.

Correction: *The birthday cake tasted sweet.*

Error: You have done good with this project.

Problem: *Good* is an adjective and cannot be used to modify a verb phrase such as have done.

Correction: *You have done well with this project.*

Error: The coach was positive happy about the team's chance of winning.

Problem: The adjective *positive* cannot be used to modify another adjective, *happy*. An adverb is needed instead.

Correction: *The coach was positively happy about the team's chance of winning.*

Error: The fireman acted quick and brave to save the child from the burning building.

Problem: *Quick and brave* are adjectives and cannot be used to describe a verb. Adverbs are needed instead.

Correction: *The fireman acted quickly and bravely to save the child from the burning building.*

PRACTICE EXERCISE: ADJECTIVES AND ADVERBS

Choose the option that corrects an error in the underlined portion(s).
If no error exists, choose "No change is necessary."

1) Moving quick throughout the house, the burglar removed several priceless antiques before carelessly dropping his wallet.

   A) quickly
   B) remove
   C) careless
   D) No change is necessary.

2) The car crashed loudly into the retaining wall before spinning wildly on the sidewalk.

   A) crashes
   B) loudly
   C) wild
   D) No change is necessary.

3) The airplane landed safe on the runway after nearly colliding with a helicopter.

   A) land
   B) safely
   C) near
   D) No change is necessary.

4) The horribly bad special effects in the movie disappointed us great.

   A) horrible
   B) badly
   C) greatly
   D) No change is necessary.

5) The man promised to faithfully obey the rules of the social club.

   A) faithful
   B) faithfulness
   C) faith
   D) No change is necessary.

TEACHER CERTIFICATION STUDY GUIDE

ANSWER KEY: PRACTICE EXERCISE FOR ADJECTIVES AND ADVERBS

1) A   The adverb *quickly* is needed to modify *moving*. Option B is incorrect because it uses the wrong form of the verb. Option C is incorrect because the adverb *carelessly* is needed before the verb *dropping,* not the adjective *careless.*

2) D   The sentence is correct as it is written. Adverbs *loudly* and *wildly* are needed to modify *crashed* and *spinning.* Option A incorrectly uses the verb *crashes* instead of the participle *crashing*, which acts as an adjective.

3) B   The adverb *safely* is needed to modify the verb *landed.* Option A is incorrect because *land* is a noun. Option C is incorrect because *near* is an adjective, not an adverb.

4) C   The adverb *greatly* is needed to modify the verb *disappointed.* Option A is incorrect because *horrible* is an adjective, not an adverb. Option B is incorrect because *bad* needs to modify the adverb *horribly.*

5) D   The adverb *faithfully* is the correct modifier of the verb *promised.* Option A is an adjective used to modify nouns. Neither Option B nor Option C, which are both nouns, is a modifier.

Skill 9.9 Logical comparisons

When comparisons are made, the correct form of the adjective or adverb must be used. The comparative form is used for two items. The superlative form is used for more than two.

	Comparative	Superlative
slow	slower	slowest
young	younger	youngest
tall	taller	tallest

With some words, *more* and *most* are used to make comparisons instead of *er* and *est*.

quiet	more quiet	most quiet
energetic	more energetic	most energetic
quick	more quickly	most quickly

Comparisons must be made between similar structures or items. In the sentence, "My house is similar in color to Steve's," one house is being compared to another house as understood by the use of the possessive *Steve's*.

On the other hand, if the sentence reads "My house is similar in color to Steve," the comparison would be faulty because it would be comparing the house to Steve, not to Steve's house.

Error: Last year's rides at the carnival were bigger than this year.

Problem: In the sentence as it is worded above, the rides at the carnival are being compared to this year, not to this year's rides.

Correction: *Last year's rides at the carnival were bigger than this year's rides.*

PRACTICE EXERCISE: LOGICAL COMPARISONS

Choose the sentence that logically and correctly expresses the comparison.

1) A. This year's standards are higher than last year.
   B. This year's standards are more high than last year.
   C. This year's standards are higher than last year's.

2) A. Tom's attitudes are very different from his father's.
   B. Toms attitudes are very different from his father.
   C. Tom's attitudes are very different from his father.

3) A. John is the stronger member of the gymnastics team.
   B. John is the strongest member of the gymnastics team.
   C. John is the most strong member of the gymnastics team.

4) A. Tracy's book report was longer than Tony's.
   B. Tracy's book report was more long than Tony's.
   C. Tracy's book report was longer than Tony.

5) A. Becoming a lawyer is as difficult as, if not more difficult than, becoming a doctor.

   B. Becoming a lawyer is as difficult, if not more difficult than, becoming a doctor.

   C. Becoming a lawyer is difficult, if not more difficult than, becoming a doctor.

6) A. Better than any movie of the modern era, Schindler's List portrays the destructiveness of hate.

   B. More better than any movie of the modern era, Schindler's List portrays the destructiveness of hate.

   C. Better than any other movie of the modern era, Schindler's List portrays the destructiveness of hate.

TEACHER CERTIFICATION STUDY GUIDE

ANSWER KEY: PRACTICE EXERCISE FOR LOGICAL COMPARISONS

1) C   Option C is correct because the comparison is between this year's standards and last year's [standards is understood]. Option A compares the standards to last year. In Option B, the faulty comparative *more high* should be *higher*.

2) A   Option A is incorrect because Tom's attitudes are compared to his father's [attitudes is understood]. Option B deletes the necessary apostrophe to show possession (Tom's), and the comparison is faulty with *attitudes* compared to father. While Option C uses the correct possessive, it retains the faulty comparison shown in Option B.

3) B   In Option B, John is correctly the strongest member of a team that consists of more than two people. Option A uses the comparative *stronger* (comparison of two items) rather than the superlative *strongest* (comparison of more than two). Option C uses a faulty superlative, *most strong*.

4) A   Option A is correct because the comparison is between Tracy's book report and Tony's (book report). Option B uses the faulty comparative *more long* instead of longer. Option C wrongly compares Tracy's book report to Tony.

5) A   In Option A, the dual comparison is correctly stated: *as difficult as, if not more difficult than*. Remember to test the dual comparison by taking out the intervening comparison. Option B deletes the necessary *as* after the first *difficult*. Option C deletes the *as* before and after the first *difficult*.

6) C   Option C includes the necessary word *other* in the comparison *better than any other movie*. The comparison in Option A is not complete, and Option B uses a faulty comparative, *more better*.

BASIC SKILLS

Skill 9.10 Identify standard spelling

Spelling correctly is not always easy because English not only utilizes an often inconsistent spelling system, but also uses many words derived from other languages. Good spelling is important because incorrect spelling damages the physical appearance of writing and may puzzle readers.

The following is a list of words that are misspelled the most often.

1. commitment
2. succeed
3. necessary
4. connected
5. opportunity
6. embarrassed
7. occasionally
8. receive
9. their
10. accelerate
11. patience
12. obstinate
13. achievement
14. responsibility
15. prejudice
16. familiar
17. hindrance
18. controversial
19. publicity
20. prescription
21. possession
22. accumulate
23. hospitality
24. judgment
25. conscious
26. height
27. leisurely
28. shield
29. foreign
30. innovative
31. similar
32. proceed
33. contemporary
34. beneficial
35. attachment
36. guarantee
37. tropical
38. misfortune
39. particular
40. yield

Spelling plurals and possessives
Spelling errors resulting from the multiplicity and complexity of spelling rules based on phonics, letter doubling, and exceptions should be addressed by consulting a good dictionary. Learning the use of a dictionary and thesaurus will be a rewarding use of time than attempting to master the bewildering forest of rules.

Most plurals of nouns that end in hard consonants or hard consonant sounds followed by a silent *e* are made by adding *s*. Some words ending in vowels only add *s*.

> fingers, numerals, banks, bugs, riots, homes, gates, radios, bananas

Nouns that end in soft consonant sounds *s, j, x, z, ch,* and *sh*, add *es*. Some nouns ending in *o* add es.

> dresses, waxes, churches, brushes, tomatoes, potatoes

Nouns ending in *y* preceded by a vowel just add *s*.

> boys, alleys

Nouns ending in *y* preceded by a consonant change the *y* to *i* and add *es*.

> babies, corollaries, frugalities, poppies

Some nouns plurals are formed irregularly or remain the same.

> sheep, deer, children, leaves, oxen

Some nouns derived from foreign words, especially Latin, may make their plurals in two different ways - one of them Anglicized. Sometimes, the meanings are the same; other times, the two plurals are used in slightly different contexts. It is always wise to consult the dictionary.

> appendices, appendixes   criterion, criteria
> indexes, indices   crisis, crises

Make the plurals of closed (solid) compound words in the usual way except for words ending in *ful* which make their plurals on the root word.

> timelines, hairpins, cupsful

Make the plurals of open or hyphenated compounds by adding the change in inflection to the word that changes in number.

> fathers-in-law, courts-martial, masters of art, doctors of medicine

Make the plurals of letters, numbers, and abbreviations by adding *s*.

fives and tens, IBMs, 1990s, *p*s and *q*s (Note that letters are italicized.)

BASIC SKILLS

I before E

i before e	grieve, fiend, niece, friend
except after c	receive, conceive, receipt
or when sounded like "a"	as in reindeer and weight, and reign
Exceptions:	weird, foreign, seize, leisure

Test on ei/ie words

Circle the correct spelling of the word in each parenthesis.

1. The (shield, shield) protected the gladiator from serious injury.
2. Tony (received, recieved) an award for his science project.
3. Our (neighbors, nieghbors), the Thomsons, are in the Witness Protection Program.
4. Janet's (friend, freind), Olivia, broke her leg while running the marathon.
5. She was unable to (conceive, concieve) a child after her miscarriage.
6. Rudolph the Red-Nosed (Riendeer, Reindeer) is my favorite Christmas song.
7. The farmer spent all day plowing his (feild, field).
8. Kat's (wieght, weight) loss plan failed, and she gained twenty pounds!
9. They couldn't (beleive, believe) how many people showed up for the concert.
10. Ruby's (niece, neice) was disappointed when the movie was sold out.

ANSWER KEY: EI/IE WORDS

1. shield
2. received
3. neighbors
4. friend
5. conceive
6. reindeer
7. field
8. weight
9. believe
10. niece

Skill 9.11 Identify standard punctuation

Commas

Commas indicate a brief pause. They are used to set off dependent clauses and long introductory word groups, to separate words in a series, to set off unimportant material that interrupts the flow of the sentence, and to separate independent clauses joined by conjunctions.

Error: After I finish my master's thesis I plan to work in Chicago.

Problem: A comma is needed after an introductory dependent word-group containing a subject and verb.

Correction: *After I finish my master's thesis, I plan to work in Chicago.*

Error: I washed waxed and vacuumed my car today.

Problem: Nouns, phrases, or clauses in a list, as well as two or more coordinate adjectives that modify one word should be separated by commas. Although the word *and* is sometimes considered optional, it is often necessary to clarify the meaning.

Correction: *I washed, waxed, and vacuumed my car today.*

Error: She was a talented dancer but she is mostly remembered for her singing ability.

Problem: A comma is needed before a conjunction that joins two independent clauses (complete sentences).

Correction: *She was a talented dancer, but she is mostly remembered for her singing ability.*

Error: This incident is I think typical of what can happen when the community remains so divided.

Problem: Commas are needed between nonessential words or words that interrupt the main clause.

Correction: *This incident is, I think, typical of what can happen when the community remains so divided.*

BASIC SKILLS

Semicolons and colons

Semicolons are needed to separate two or more closely related independent clauses when the second clause is introduced by a transitional adverb. (These clauses may also be written as separate sentences, preferably by placing the adverb within the second sentence).

Colons are used to introduce lists and to emphasize what follows.

Error: I climbed to the top of the mountain, it took me three hours.

Problem: A comma alone cannot separate two independent clauses. Instead a semicolon is needed to separate two related sentences.

Correction: *I climbed to the top of the mountain; it took me three hours.*

Error: In the movie, asteroids destroyed Dallas, Texas, Kansas City, Missouri, and Boston, Massachusetts.

Problem: Semicolons are needed to separate items in a series that already contains internal punctuation.

Correction: *In the movie, asteroids destroyed Dallas, Texas; Kansas City, Missouri; and Boston, Massachusetts.*

Error: Essays will receive the following grades, A for excellent, B for good, C for average, and D for unsatisfactory.

Problem: A colon is needed to emphasize the information or list that follows.

Correction: *Essays will receive the following grades: A for excellent, B for good, C for average, and D for unsatisfactory.*

Error: The school carnival included: amusement rides, clowns, food booths, and a variety of games.

Problem: The material preceding the colon and the list that follows is not a complete sentence. Do not separate a verb (or preposition) from the object.

Correction: *The school carnival included amusement rides, clowns, food booths, and a variety of games.*

Apostrophes

Apostrophes are used to show either contractions or possession.

Error: She shouldnt be permitted to smoke cigarettes in the building.

Problem: An apostrophe is needed in a contraction in place of the missing letter.

Correction: *She shouldn't be permitted to smoke cigarettes in the building.*

Error: My cousins motorcycle was stolen from his driveway.

Problem: An apostrophe is needed to show possession.

Correction: *My cousin's motorcycle was stolen from his driveway.* (Note: The use of the apostrophe before the letter "s" means that there is just one cousin. The plural form would read the following way: My cousins' motorcycle was stolen from their driveway.)

Error: The childrens new kindergarten teacher was also a singer.

Problem: An apostrophe is needed to show possession.

Correction: *The children's new kindergarten teacher was also a singer.* (Note: *Children* is plural, the singular of which is *child*.)

Error: Children screams could be heard for miles.

Problem: An apostrophe and the letter s are needed in the sentence to show whose screams it is.

Correction: *Children's screams could he heard for miles.* (Note: Because the word children is already plural, the apostrophe and *s* denote ownership.)

Quotation marks

In a quoted statement that is either declarative or imperative, place the period inside the closing quotation marks.

"The airplane crashed on the runway during takeoff."

If the quotation is followed by other words in the sentence, place a comma inside the closing quotations marks and a period at the end of the sentence.

"The airplane crashed on the runway during takeoff," said the announcer.

In most instances in which a quoted title or expression occurs at the end of a sentence, the period is placed before either the single or double quotation marks.

"The middle school readers were unprepared to understand Bryant's poem 'Thanatopsis.'"

Early book-length adventure stories like *Don Quixote* and *The Three Musketeers* were known as "picaresque novels."

There is an instance in which the final quotation mark would precede the period—if the content of the sentence were about a speech or quote so that the understanding of the meaning would be confused by the placement of the period.

The first thing out of his mouth was "Hi, I'm home."
but
The first line of his speech began "I arrived home to an empty house".

In sentences that are interrogatory or exclamatory, the question mark or exclamation point should be positioned outside the closing quotation marks if the quote itself is a statement or command or cited title.

Who decided to lead us in the recitation of the "Pledge of Allegiance"?

Why was Tillie shaking as she began her recitation, "Once upon a midnight dreary..."?

I was embarrassed when Mrs. White said, "Your slip is showing"!

In sentences that are declarative but that contain a quotation that is a question or an exclamation, place the question mark or exclamation point inside the quotation marks.

The hall monitor yelled, "Fire! Fire!"

"Fire! Fire!" yelled the hall monitor.

Cory shrieked, "Is there a mouse in the room?" (In this instance, the question supersedes the exclamation.)

Quotations - whether words, phrases, or clauses - should be punctuated according to the rules of the grammatical function they serve in the sentence.

The works of Shakespeare, "the Bard of Avon," have been contested as originating with other authors.

"You'll get my money," the old man warned, "when 'Hell freezes over'."

Sheila cited the passage that began "Four score and seven years ago...." (Note the ellipsis followed by an enclosed period.)

"Old Ironsides" inspired the preservation of the U.S.S. Constitution. Use quotation marks to enclose the titles of shorter works: songs, short poems, short stories, essays, and chapters of books. (See "Using Italics" for punctuating longer titles.)

"The Tell-Tale Heart"   "Casey at the Bat"   "America the Beautiful"

Dashes and Italics

Place **dashes** to denote sudden breaks in thought.

Some periods in literature - the Romantic Age, for example - spanned different time periods in different countries.

Use dashes instead of commas if commas are already used elsewhere in the sentence for amplification or explanation.

The Fireside Poets included three Brahmans - James Russell Lowell, Henry David Wadsworth, Oliver Wendell Holmes - and John Greenleaf Whittier.

Use **italics** to punctuate the titles of long works of literature, names of periodical publications; musical scores; works of art; and motion picture, television, and radio programs. (When unable to write in italics, students should be instructed to underline in their own writing where italics would be appropriate.)

The Idylls of the King   *Hiawatha*   *The Sound and the Fury*
Mary Poppins   *Newsweek*   *The Nutcracker Suite*

Skill 9.12 Identify standard capitalization

Capitalize all proper names of persons (including specific organizations or agencies of government); places (countries, states, cities, parks, and specific geographical areas); and things (political parties, structures, historical and cultural terms, and calendar and time designations); and religious terms (any deity, revered person or group, and sacred writings).

> Percy Bysshe Shelley, Argentina, Mount Rainier National Park, Grand Canyon, League of Nations, the Sears Tower, Birmingham, Lyric Theater, Americans, Midwesterners, Democrats, Renaissance, Boy Scouts of America, Easter, God, Bible, Dead Sea Scrolls, Koran

Capitalize proper adjectives and titles used with proper names.

California gold rush, President John Adams, French fries, Homeric epic, Romanesque architecture, Senator John Glenn

Note: Some words that represent titles and offices are not capitalized unless used with a proper name.

Capitalized	Not Capitalized
Congressman McKay	the congressman from Florida
Commander Alger	commander of the Pacific Fleet
Queen Elizabeth	the queen of England

Capitalize all main words in titles of works of literature, art, and music.

Error: Emma went to Dr. Peters for treatment since her own Doctor was on vacation.

Problem: The use of capital letters with *Emma* and *Dr .Peters* is correct since they are specific (proper) names; the title *Dr.* is also capitalized. However, the word *doctor* is not a specific name and should not be capitalized.

Correction: *Emma went to Dr. Peters for treatment since her own doctor was on vacation.*

Error: Our Winter Break does not start until next wednesday.

Problem: Days of the week are capitalized, but seasons are not capitalized.

Correction: *Our winter break does not start until next Wednesday.*

Error: The exchange student from israel who came to study biochemistry spoke spanish very well.

Problem: Languages and the names of countries are always capitalized. Courses are also capitalized when they refer to a specific course; they are not capitalized when they refer to courses in general.

Correction: *The exchange student from Israel who came to study Biochemistry spoke Spanish very well.*

TEACHER CERTIFICATION STUDY GUIDE

PRACTICE EXERCISE: CAPITALIZATION AND PUNCTUALIZATION

Choose the option that corrects an error in the underlined portion(s). If no error exists, choose "No change is necessary".

1) Greenpeace is an Organization that works to preserve the world's environment.

   A) greenpeace
   B) organization
   C) worlds
   D) No change is necessary

2) When our class travels to France next year, we will see the country's many famous landmarks.

   A) france
   B) year; we
   C) countries
   D) No change is necessary

3) New York City, the heaviest populated city in America has more than eight million people living there everyday.

   A) new york city
   B) in America, has
   C) Everyday
   D) No change is necessary

4) The television show The X-Files has gained a huge following because it focuses on paranormal phenomena, extraterrestrial life, and the oddities of human existence.

   A) Television
   B) following, because
   C) Human existence
   D) No change is necessary

BASIC SKILLS

5) Being a Policeman requires having many qualities: physical agility, good reflexes, and the ability to make quick decisions.

   A) policeman
   B) qualities;
   C) agility:
   D) No change is necessary

6) "Better to have loved and lost than never to have loved at all," says the writer, who demonstrates the value of love in a mans life.

   A) Better to have loved and lost, than never to have loved at all
   B) writer who
   C) man's
   D) No change is necessary

7) The Florida Marlins won the world Series championship by defeating the New York Mets in October 1996.

   A) Florida marlins
   B) World Series
   C) October,1996
   D) No change is necessary

ANSWER KEY: PRACTICE EXERCISE FOR CAPITALIZATION AND PUNCTUATION

1. B In the sentence, the word *organization* does not need to be capitalized, due to the fact that it is a general noun. In Option A, the name of the organization should be capitalized. In Option C, the apostrophe is used to show that one world is being protected, not more than one.

2. D In Option A, *France* is capitalized because it is the name of a country. In Option B, the comma, not the semi-colon, should separate a dependent clause from the main clause. In Option C, the use of an apostrophe and an *s* indicates only one country is being visited.

3. B In Option A, *New York City* is capitalized because it is the name of a place. In Option B, a comma is needed to separate the noun *America*, from the verb *has*. In Option C, the noun *everyday* needs no capitalization.

4. D In Option A, *television* does not need to be capitalized because it is a noun. In Option B, a comma is necessary to separate an independent clause from the main clause. In Option C, *human existence* is a general term that does not need capitalization.

5. A In Option A, *policeman* does not need capitalization because it is a general noun. In Option B, a colon, not a semi-colon, is needed because the rest of the sentence is related to the main clause. In Option C, a comma, not a colon, is needed to separate the adjectives.

6. C In Option A, a comma is needed to break the quote into distinct parts that give it a greater clarity. In Option B, a comma is needed to separate the subject of the sentence from his action. In Option C, an apostrophe is needed to show possession.

7. B In Option A, *Florida Marlins* must be capitalized because it is the name of a team. In Option B, *World Series* needs to be capitalized because it is the title of a sporting event. In Option C, no comma is needed because *month* and *year* need no distinction; they are general terms.

Sample Test I: English

DIRECTIONS : *The passage below contains many errors. Read the passage. Then answer each test item by choosing the option that corrects an error in the underlined portion(s). No more than one underlined error will appear in each item. If no error exists, choose "No change is necessary."*

Climbing to the top of Mount Everest is an adventure. One which everyone--whether physically fit or not--seems eager to try. The trail stretches for miles, the cold temperatures are usually frigid and brutal.

Climbers must endure severel barriers on the way, including other hikers, steep jagged rocks, and lots of snow. Plus, climbers often find the most grueling part of the trip is their climb back down, just when they are feeling greatly exhausted. Climbers who take precautions are likely to find the ascent less arduous than the unprepared. By donning heavy flannel shirts, gloves, and hats, climbers prevented hypothermia, as well as simple frostbite. A pair of rugged boots is also one of the necesities. If climbers are to avoid becoming dehydrated, there is beverages available for them to transport as well.

Once climbers are completely ready to begin their lengthy journey, they can comfortable enjoy the wonderful scenery. Wide rock formations dazzle the observers eyes with shades of gray and white, while the peak forms a triangle that seems to touch the sky. Each of the climbers are reminded of the splendor and magnifisence of Gods great Earth.

1) **Climbing to the top of Mount Everest is an adventure. One which everyone —whether physically fit or not— seems eager to try.**

   A. adventure, one
   B. people, whether
   C. seem
   D. No change is necessary

2) **The trail stretches for miles, the cold temperatures are usually frigid and brutal.**

   A. trails
   B. miles;
   C. usual
   D. No change is necessary

3) **Climbers must endure severel barriers on the way, including other hikers, steep jagged rocks, and lots of snow.**

   A. several
   B. on the way: including
   C. hikers'
   D. No change is necessary

4) Plus, climbers often find the most grueling part of the trip is **their** climb back **down, just** when they **are** feeling greatly exhausted.

   A. his
   B. down; just
   C. were
   D. No change is necessary

5) **Climbers who** take precautions are likely to find the ascent **less difficult than** the unprepared.

   A. Climbers, who
   B. least difficult
   C. then
   D. No change is necessary

6) By donning heavy flannel shirts, boots, and **hats, climbers prevented** hypothermia, as well as simple frostbite.

   A. hats climbers
   B. can prevent
   C. hypothermia;
   D. No change is necessary

7) A pair of rugged boots **is also one** of the **necesities**.

   A. are
   B. also, one
   C. necessities
   D. No change is necessary

8) If climbers are to avoid **becoming** dehydrated, there **is** beverages available for **them** to transport as well.

   A. becomming
   B. are
   C. him
   D. No change is necessary

9) Once climbers are completely prepared for **their** lengthy **journey, they** can **comfortable** enjoy the wonderful scenery.

   A. they're
   B. journey; they
   C. comfortably
   D. No change is necessary

10) Wide rock formations dazzle the **observers eyes** with shades of gray and **white, while** the peak **forms** a triangle that seems to touch the sky.

    A. observers' eyes
    B. white; while
    C. formed
    D. No change is necessary

11) Each of the climbers **are** reminded of the splendor and **magnifisence** of **God's** great Earth.

    A. is
    B. magnifisence
    C. Gods
    D. No change is necessary

DIRECTIONS: *The passage below contains several errors. Read the passage. Then answer each test item by choosing the option that corrects an error in the underlined portion(s). No more than one underlined error will appear in each item. If no error exists, choose "No change is necessary."*

Every job places different kinds of demands on their employees. For example, whereas such jobs as accounting and bookkeeping require mathematical ability; graphic design requires creative/artistic ability.
Doing good at one job does not usually guarantee success at another. However, one of the elements crucial to all jobs are especially notable: the chance to accomplish a goal.
The accomplishment of the employees varies according to the job. In many jobs the employees become accustom to the accomplishment provided by the work they do every day.
In medicine, for example, every doctor tests him self by treating badly injured or critically ill people. In the operating room, a team of Surgeons, is responsible for operating on many of these patients. In addition to the feeling of accomplishment that the workers achieve, some jobs also give a sense of identity to the employees'. Profesions like law, education, and sales offer huge financial and emotional rewards. Politicians are public servants: who work for the federal and state governments. President bush is basically employed by the American people to make laws and run the country.

Finally; the contributions that employees make to their companies and to the world cannot be taken for granted. Through their work, employees are performing a service for their employers and are contributing something to the world.

12) Every job <u>places</u> different kinds of demands on <u>their employees</u>.

   A. place
   B. its
   C. employes
   D. No change is necessary

13) <u>For example, whereas</u> such jobs as accounting and bookkeeping require mathematical <u>ability;</u> graphic design requires creative/artistic ability.

   A. For example
   B. whereas,
   C. ability,
   D. No change is necessary

14) Doing <u>good</u> at one job does not <u>usually</u> guarantee <u>success</u> at another.

   A. well
   B. usualy
   C. succeeding
   D. No change is necessary

15) However, one of the elements crucial to all jobs are especially notable: the accomplishment of a goal.

   A. However
   B. is
   C. notable;
   D. No change is necessary

16) The accomplishment of the employees varies according to the job.

   A. accomplishment,
   B. employee's
   C. vary
   D. No change is necessary

17) In many jobs the employees become accustom to the accomplishment provided by the work they do every day.

   A. became
   B. accustomed
   C. provides
   D. No change is necessary

18) In medicine, for example, every doctor tests him self by treating badly injured and critically ill people.

   A. test
   B. himself
   C. critical
   D. No change is necessary

19) In the operating room, a team of Surgeons, is responsible for operating on many of these patients.

   A. operating room:
   B. surgeons is
   C. those
   D. No change is necessary

20) In addition to the feeling of accomplishment that the workers achieve, some jobs also give a sense of self-identity to the employees'.

   A. acheive
   B. gave
   C. employees
   D. No change is necessary

21) Profesions like law, education, and sales offer huge financial and emotional rewards.

   A. Professions
   B. education;
   C. offered
   D. No change is necessary

22) Politicians are public servants: who work for the federal and state governments.

   A. were
   B. servants who
   C. worked
   D. No change is necessary

GENERAL KNOWLEDGE

23) President bush is basically employed <u>by</u> the American people to <u>make</u> laws and run the country.

   A. Bush
   B. to
   C. made
   D. No change is necessary

24) <u>Finally;</u> the contributions that employees make to <u>their</u> companies and to the world cannot be <u>taken</u> for granted.

   A. Finally,
   B. their
   C. took
   D. No change is necessary

DIRECTIONS: *For the underlined sentence(s), choose the option that expresses the meaning with the most fluency and the clearest logic within the context. If the underlined sentence should not be changed, choose Option A, which shows no change.*

25) Selecting members of a President's cabinet can often be an aggravating process. <u>Either there are too many or too few qualified candidates for a certain position, and then they have to be confirmed by the Senate, where there is the possibility of rejection.</u>

   A. Either there are too many or too few qualified candidate for a certain position, and then they have to be confirmed by the Senate, where there is the possibility of rejection.

   B. Qualified candidates for certain positions face the possibility of rejection, when they have to be confirmed by the Senate.

   C. The Senate has to confirm qualified candidates, who face the possibility of rejection.

   D. Because the Senate has to confirm qualified candidates; they face the possibility of rejection.

26) Treating patients for drug and/or alcohol abuse is a sometimes difficult process. <u>Even though there are a number of different methods for helping the patient overcome a dependency, there is no way of knowing which is best in the long-run.</u>

A. Even though there are a number of different methods for helping the patient overcome a dependency, there is no way of knowing which is best in the long-run.

B. Even though different methods can help a patient overcome a dependency, there is no way to know which is best in the long-run.

C. Even though there is no way to know which way is best in the long run, patients can overcome their dependencies when they are helped.

D. There is no way to know which method will help the patient overcome a dependency in the long-run, even though there are many different ones.

27) Many factors account for the decline in quality of public education. <u>Overcrowding, budget cutbacks, and societal deterioration which have greatly affected student learning.</u>

A. Overcrowding, budget cutbacks, and societal deterioration which have greatly affected student learning.

B. Student learning has been greatly affected by overcrowding, budget cutbacks, and societal deterioration.

C. Due to overcrowding, budget cutbacks, and societal deterioration, student learning has been greatly affected.

D. Overcrowding, budget cutbacks, and societal deterioration have affected students learning greatly.

DIRECTIONS: *Choose the sentence that logically and correctly expresses the comparison.*

28) A. The Empire State Building in New York is taller than buildings in the city.

B. The Empire State Building in New York is taller than any other building in the city.

C. The Empire State Building in New York is tallest than other buildings in the city.

DIRECTIONS: *Choose the most effective word within the context of the sentence.*

29) Many of the clubs in Boca Raton are noted for their _____ elegance.

A. vulgar
B. tasteful
C. ordinary

30) When a student is expelled from school, the parents are usually _____ in advance.

A. rewarded
B. congratulated
C. notified

31) Before appearing in court, the witness was _____ the papers requiring her to show up.

A. condemned
B. served
C. criticized

DIRECTIONS: *Choose the underlined word or phrase that is unnecessary within the context of the passage.*

32) <u>Considered by many to be</u> one of the worst <u>terrorist</u> incidents <u>on American soil</u> was the bombing of the Oklahoma City Federal Building which will be remembered <u>for years to come</u>.

A. considered by many to be
B. terrorist
C. on American soil
D. for years to come

33) The <u>flu</u> epidemic struck <u>most of</u> the <u>respected</u> faculty and students of The Woolbright School, forcing the Boynton Beach School Superintendent to close It down <u>for two weeks.</u>

A. flu
B. most of
C. respected
D. for two weeks

34) The <u>expanding</u> number of television channels has <u>prompted</u> cable operators to raise their prices, <u>even though</u> many consumers do not want to pay a higher <u>increased</u> amount for their service.

A. expanding
B. prompted
C. even though
D. increased

GENERAL KNOWLEDGE

DIRECTIONS: *The passage below contains several errors. Read the passage. Then answer each test item by choosing the option that corrects an error in the underlined portion(s). No more than one underlined error will appear in each item. If no error exists, choose "No change is necessary."*

The discovery of a body at Paris Point marina in Boca Raton shocked the residents of Palmetto Pines, a luxury condominium complex located next door to the marina.

The victim is a thirty-five year old woman who had been apparently bludgeoned to death and dumped in the ocean late last night. Many neighbors reported terrible screams, gunshots: as well as the sound of a car backfiring loudly to Boca Raton Police shortly after midnight. The woman had been spotted in the lobby of Palmetto Pines around ten thirty, along with an older man, estimated to be in his fifties, and a younger man, in his late twenties.

"Apparently, the victim had been driven to the complex by the older man, and was seen arguing with him when the younger man intervened", said Sheriff Fred Adams, "all three of them left the building together and walked to the marina, where gunshots rang out an hour later." Deputies found five bullets on the sidewalk and some blood, along with a steel pipe that is assumed to be the murder weapon. Two men were seen fleeing the scene in a red Mercedes short after, rushing toward the Interstate.

The Palm Beach County Coroner, Melvin Watts, said he concluded the victim's skull had been crushed by a blunt tool, which resulted in a brain hemorrhage. As of now, there is no clear motive for the murder.

35) **The discovery of a body at Paris Point marina in Boca Raton shocked the residents of Palmetto Pines, a luxury condominium complex located next door to the marina.**

   A. Marina
   B. residence
   C. condominium
   D. No change is necessary

36) **The victim is a thirty-five year old who had been apparently bludgeoned to death and dumped in the ocean late last night.**

   A. was
   B. bludgoned
   C. ocean: late
   D. No change is necessary

37) **Many neighbors reported terrible screams, gunshots: as well as the sound of a car backfiring loudly to Boca Raton Police shortly after midnight.**

   A. nieghbors
   B. gunshots, as
   C. loud
   D. No change is necessary

GENERAL KNOWLEDGE

38) The woman had been spotted in the lobby of Palmetto Pines around ten thirty, along with an older man, estimated to be in his fifties, and a younger man in his late twenties.

A. has
B. thirty;
C. man estimated
D. No change is necessary

39) "Apparently, the victim had been driven to the complex by the older man, and was seen arguing with him when the younger man intervened," said Sheriff Fred Adams, "all three of them left the building together and walked to the marina, when gunshots rang out an hour later."

A. sheriff Fred Adams, "all
B. sheriff Fred Adams, "All
C. Sheriff Fred Adams." All
D. No change is necessary

40) Deputies found five bullets on the sidewalk and some blood, along with a steel pipe that is assumed to be the murder weapon.

A. blood;
B. assuming
C. to have been
D. No change is necessary

41) Two men were seen fleeing the scene in a red Mercedes short after, rushing toward the Interstate.

A. are
B. shortly
C. rushed
D. No change is necessary

42) The Palm Beach County Coroner, Kelvin Watts, said he concluded the victim's skull had been crushed by a blunt tool, which resulted in a brain hemorrhage.

A. palm beach
B. coroner
C. hemorrhage
D. No change is necessary

43) As of now, there is no clear motive for the murder.

A. now;
B. their
C. was
D. No change is necessary

DIRECTIONS: *Choose the most effective word or phrase within the context suggested by the sentence.*

44) Because George's _____ bothering him, he apologized for crashing his father's car.

   A. feelings were
   B. conscience was
   C. guiltiness was

45) The charity art auction _____ every year at Mizner Park has a wide selection of artists showcasing their work.

   A. attended
   B. presented
   C. displayed

DIRECTIONS: *For the underlined sentence(s), choose the option that expresses the meaning with the most fluency and the clearest logic within the context. If the underlined sentence should not be changed, choose Option A, which shows no change.*

46) John wanted to join his friends on the mountain-climbing trip. <u>Seeing that the weather had become dark and stormy, John knew he would stay safe indoors.</u>

   A. Seeing that the weather had become dark and stormy, John knew he would stay safe indoors.

   B. The weather had become dark and stormy, and John knew he would stay indoors, and he would be safe.

   C. Because the weather had become dark and stormy, John knew he would stay indoors, where he would be safe.

   D. Because the weather had become dark, as well as stormy, John knew he would stay safe indoors.

47) A few hours later, the storm subsided, so John left the cabin to join his friends. **Even though he was tired from the four-mile hike the day before; he climbed the mountain in a few hours.**

   A. Even though he was tired from the four-mile hike the day before, he climbed the mountain in a few hours.

   B. He was tired from the four-mile hike the day four-mile hike the day before; he climbed the mountain in a few hours.

   C. He climbed the mountain in a few hours, John was tired from the four-mile hike the day before.

   D. Seeing as he was tired from the day before, when he went on a four-mile hike, John climbed the mountain in a few hours.

Answer Key: English

1. A
2. B
3. A
4. D
5. D
6. B
7. C
8. B
9. C
10. A
11. A
12. B
13. C
14. A
15. B
16. C
17. B
18. B
19. B
20. C
21. A
22. B
23. A
24. A
25. C
26. B
27. B
28. B
29. B
30. C
31. B
32. A
33. C
34. D
35. A
36. A
37. B
38. C
39. C
40. C
41. B
42. C
43. D
44. B
45. B
46. D
47. A

TEACHER CERTIFICATION STUDY GUIDE

Rationales for Sample Questions: English

1. **A** A comma is needed between *adventure* and *one* to avoid creating a fragment of the second part. In Option B, a comma after *everyone* would not be appropriate when the dash is used on the other side of *not*. In Option C, the singular verb *seems* is needed to agree with the singular subject *everyone*.

2. **B** A semicolon, not a comma, is needed to separate the first independent clause from the second independent clause. Option A is incorrect because the plural subject *trails* needs the singular verb stretch. Option C is incorrect because the adverb form *usually* is needed to modify the adjective *frigid*.

3. **A** The word *several* is misspelled in the text. Option B is incorrect because a comma, not a colon, is needed to set off the modifying phrase. Option C is incorrect because no apostrophe is needed after *hikers* since possession is not involved.

4. **D** The present tense must be used consistently throughout, therefore Option C is incorrect. Option A is incorrect because the singular pronoun *his* does not agree with the plural antecedent *climbers*. Option B is incorrect because a comma, not a semicolon, is needed to separate the dependent clause from the main clause.

5. **D** No change is needed. Option A is incorrect because a comma would make the phrase *who take precautions* seem less restrictive or less essential to the sentence. Option B is incorrect because *less* is appropriate when two items--the prepared and the unprepared--are compared. Option C is incorrect because the comparative adverb *than*, not *then*, is needed.

6. **B** The verb *prevented* is in the past tense and must be changed to the present *can prevent* to be consistent. Option A is incorrect because a comma is needed after a long introductory phrase. Option C is incorrect because the semicolon creates a fragment of the phrase *as well as simple frostbite*.

7. **C** The word *necessities* is misspelled in the text. Option A is incorrect because the singular verb is must agree with the singular noun *pair* (a collective singular). Option B is incorrect because *if also* is set off with commas (potential correction), it should be set off on both sides.

8. **B** The plural verb *are* must be used with the plural subject *beverages*. Option A is incorrect because *becoming* has only one m. Option C is incorrect because the plural pronoun *them* is needed to agree with the referent *climbers*.

GENERAL KNOWLEDGE

9. **C** The adverb form *comfortably* is needed to modify the verb phrase *can enjoy*. Option A is incorrect because the possessive plural pronoun is spelled *their*. Option B is incorrect because a semicolon would make the first half of the item seem like an independent clause when the subordinating conjunction *once* makes that clause dependent.

10. **A** An apostrophe is needed to show the plural possessive form *observers' eyes*. Option B is incorrect because the semicolon would make the second half of the item seem like an independent clause when the subordinating conjunction *while* makes that clause dependent. Option C is incorrect because *formed* is in the wrong tense.

11. **A** The singular verb *is* agrees with the singular subject *each*. Option B is incorrect because *magnificence* is misspelled. Option C is incorrect because an apostrophe is needed to show possession.

12. **B** The singular possessive pronoun *its* must agree with its antecedent *job*, which is singular also. Option A is incorrect because *place* is a plural form and the subject, *job*, is singular. Option C is incorrect because the correct spelling of *employees* is given in the sentence.

13. **C** An introductory dependent clause is set off with a comma, not a semicolon. Option A is incorrect because the transitional phrase *for example* should be set off with a comma. Option B is incorrect because the adverb *whereas* functions like *while* and does not take a comma after it.

14. **A** The adverb *well* modifies the word *doing*. Option B is incorrect because *usually* is spelled correctly in the sentence. Option C is incorrect because *succeeding* is in the wrong tense.

15. **B** The singular verb *is* is needed to agree with the singular subject *one*. Option A is incorrect because a comma is needed to set off the transitional word *however*. Option C is incorrect because a colon, not a semicolon, is needed to set off an item.

16. **C** The singular verb *vary* is needed to agree with the singular subject *accomplishment*. Option A is incorrect because a comma after *accomplishment* would suggest that the modifying phrase *of the employees* is additional instead of essential. Option B is incorrect because *employees* is not possessive.

17. **B** The past participle *accustomed* is needed with the verb *become*. Option A is incorrect because the verb tense does not need to change to the past *became*. Option C is incorrect because *provides* is the wrong tense.

TEACHER CERTIFICATION STUDY GUIDE

18. **B** The reflexive pronoun *himself* is needed. (Him self is nonstandard and never correct.) Option A is incorrect because the singular verb test is needed to agree with the singular subject doctor. Option C is incorrect because the adverb *critically* is needed to modify the verb *ill*.

19. **B** *Surgeons* is not a proper name so it does not need to be capitalized. A comma is not needed to break up *a team of surgeons* from the rest of the sentence. Option A is incorrect because a comma, not a colon, is needed to set off an item. Option C is incorrect because *those* is an incorrect pronoun.

20. **C** Option C is correct because *employees* is not possessive. Option A is incorrect because *achieve* is spelled correctly in the sentence. Option B is incorrect because *gave* is the wrong tense.

21. **A** Option A is correct because *professions* is misspelled in the sentence. Option B is incorrect because a comma, not a semi-colon, is needed after *education*. In Option C, *offered*, is in the wrong tense.

22. **B** A colon is not needed to set off the introduction of the sentence. In Option A, *were*, is the incorrect tense of the verb. In Option C, *worked*, is in the wrong tense.

23. **A** *Bush* is a proper name and should be capitalized. Option B, *to*, does not fit with the verb *employed*. Option C uses the wrong form of the verb, *make*.

24. **A** A comma is needed to separate *Finally* from the rest of the sentence. Finally is a preposition which usually heads a dependent sentence, hence a comma is needed. Option B is incorrect because *their* is misspelled. Option C is incorrect because *took* is the wrong form of the verb.

25. **C** Option C is the most straightforward and concise sentence. Option A is too unwieldy with the wordy *Either...or* phrase at the beginning. Option B doesn't make clear the fact that candidates face rejection by the Senate. Option D illogically implies that candidates face rejection because they have to be confirmed by the Senate.

26. **B** Option B is concise and logical. Option A tends to ramble with the use of *there are* and the verbs *helping* and *knowing*. Option C is awkwardly worded and repetitive in the first part of the sentence, and vague in the second because it never indicates how the patients can be helped. Option D contains the unnecessary phrase *even though there are many different ones*.

GENERAL KNOWLEDGE

TEACHER CERTIFICATION STUDY GUIDE

27. **B** Option B is concise and best explains the causes of the decline in student education. The unnecessary use of *which* in Option A makes the sentence feel incomplete. Option C has weak coordination between the reasons for the decline in public education and the fact that student learning has been affected. Option D incorrectly places the adverb *greatly* after learning, instead of before *affected*.

28. **B** Because the Empire State Building is a building in New York City, the phrase *any other* must be included. Option A is incorrect because the Empire State Building is implicitly compared to itself since it is one of the buildings. Option C is incorrect because *tallest* is the incorrect form of the adjective.

29. **B** *Tasteful* means beautiful or charming, which would correspond to an elegant club. The words *vulgar* and *ordinary* have negative connotations.

30. **C** *Notified* means informed or told, which fits into the logic of the sentence. The words *rewarded* and *congratulated* are positive actions, which don't make sense regarding someone being expelled from school.

31. **B** *Served* means given, which makes sense in the context of the sentence. *Condemned* and *criticized* do not make sense within the context of the sentence.

32. **A** *Considered by many to be* is a wordy phrase and unnecessary in the context of the sentence. All other words are necessary within the context of the sentence.

33. **C** The fact that the faculty might have been *respected* is not really necessary to mention in the sentence. The other words and phrases are all necessary to complete the meaning of the sentence.

34. **D** The word *increased* is redundant with *higher* and should be removed. All the other words are necessary within the context of the sentence.

35. **A.** *Marina* is a name that needs to be capitalized. Options B and C create misspellings.

36. **A.** The past tense *was* is needed to maintain consistency. Option B creates a misspelling. Option C incorrectly uses a colon when none is needed.

37. **B** Option B correctly uses a comma, not a colon to separate the items. Option A creates a misspelling. Option C incorrectly changes the adverb into an adjective.

38. **C.** A comma is not needed to separate the item because *an older man estimated to be in his fifties* is one complete fragment. Option A incorrectly uses the present tense *has* instead of the past tense *had*. Option B incorrectly uses a colon when a comma is needed.

39. **C** The quote's source comes in the middle of two independent clauses, so a period should follow *Adams*. Option A is incorrect because titles, when they come before a name, must be capitalized. Punctuation is also faulty. Option B is incorrect because the word *Adams* ends a sentence; a comma is not strong enough to support two sentences.

40. **C** The past tense *to have been* is needed to maintain consistency. Option A incorrectly uses a colon, instead of a comma. Option B uses the wrong form of the verb *assumed.*

41. **B** The adverb *shortly* is needed instead of the adjective short. Option A incorrectly uses the present tense *are* instead of the past tense *were*. Option C, *rushed*, is the wrong form of the verb.

42. **C** Option C uses the correct spelling of *hemorrhage*. Option A is incorrect because *Palm Beach* is a proper name and needs to be capitalized. Option B incorrectly uses a colon when a comma is needed to separate the items.

43. **D** Option A is incorrect because a comma is needed to separate the independent clause from the dependent clause. Option B creates a misspelling. Option C uses the incorrect tense, *was*, which doesn't fit with the present tense phrase *as of now*.

44. **B** Option B shows the correct word choice because a *conscience* would motivate someone to confess. Option A is incorrect because *feelings* is not as accurate as conscience. Option C is incorrect because *guiltiness* is less descriptive of George's motive for confession than conscience.

45. **B** The word *presented* makes the most sense in the context of the sentence than *attended* or *displayed*

46. **D** This sentence best subordinates the idea of dark and stormy weather to John's knowledge. Option A is incorrect because *seeing that* is an awkward construction. Option B does not subordinate any idea to any other. Option C is incorrect because the idea that John would be safe shouldn't be subordinate to staying indoors.

47. **A** The idea that John was tired from the four-mile hike the day before is subordinate to the idea of John climbing the mountain. Options B and C do not subordinate the idea of John being tired from the four-mile hike to John climbing the mountain. In Option D, the modifying phrase *Seeing as... before* makes no logical sense in the context of the sentence.

DOMAIN III. READING

COMPETENCY 10.0 KNOWLEDGE OF LITERAL COMPREHENSION

Skill 10.1 Recognize main ideas

The main idea of a passage or paragraph is the basic message, idea, point concept, or meaning that the author wants to convey to you, the reader. Understanding the main idea of a passage or paragraph is the key to understanding the more subtle components of the author's message. The main idea is what is being said about a topic or subject. Once you have identified the basic message, you will have an easier time answering other questions that test critical skills.

Main ideas are either *stated* or *implied*. A *stated main idea* is explicit: it is directly expressed in a sentence or two in the paragraph or passage. An *implied main idea* is suggested by the overall reading selection. In the first case, you need not pull information from various points in the paragraph or passage in order to form the main idea because it is already stated by the author. If a main idea is implied, however, you must formulate, in your own words, a main idea statement by condensing the overall message contained in the material itself.

Practice Question: Read the following passage and select an answer

Sometimes too much of a good thing can become a very bad thing indeed. In an earnest attempt to consume a healthy diet, dietary supplement enthusiasts have been known to overdose. Vitamin C, for example, long thought to help people ward off cold viruses, is currently being studied for its possible role in warding off cancer and other disease that cases tissue degeneration. Unfortunately, an overdose of vitamin C – more than 10,000 mg – on a daily basis can cause nausea and diarrhea. Calcium supplements, commonly taken by women, are helpful in warding off osteoporosis. More than just a few grams a day, however, can lead to stomach upset and even kidney and bladder stones. Niacin, proven useful in reducing cholesterol levels, can be dangerous in large doses to those who suffer from heart problems, asthma or ulcers.

The main idea expressed in this paragraph is:

    A.   supplements taken in excess can be a bad thing indeed
    B.   dietary supplement enthusiasts have been known to overdose
    C.   vitamins can cause nausea, diarrhea, and kidney or bladder stones.
    D.   people who take supplements are preoccupied with their health.

Answer: Answer A is a paraphrase of the first sentence and provides a general framework for the rest of the paragraph: excess supplement intake is bad. The rest of the paragraph discusses the consequences of taking too many vitamins. Options B and C refer to major details and Option D introduces the idea of preoccupation, which is not included in this paragraph.

Skill 10.2   Identify supporting details

Supporting details are examples, facts, ideas, illustrations, cases and anecdotes used by a writer to explain, expand upon, and develop the more general main idea. A writer's choice of supporting materials is determined by the nature of the topic being covered. Supporting details are specifics that relate directly to the main idea. Writers select and shape material according to their purposes. An advertisement writer seeking to persuade the reader to buy a particular running shoe, for instance will emphasize only the positive characteristics of the shoe for advertisement copy. A columnist for a running magazine, on the other hand, might list the good and bad points about the same shoe in an article recommending appropriate shoes for different kind of runners. Both major details (those that directly support the main idea), and minor details (those that provide interesting, but not always essential, information) help create a well-written and fluid passage.

In the following paragraph, the sentences in **bold print** provide a skeleton of a paragraph on the benefits of recycling. The sentences in bold are generalizations that by themselves do not explain the need to recycle. The sentences in *italics* add details to SHOW the general points in bold. Notice how the supporting details help you understand the necessity for recycling.

While one day recycling may become mandatory in all states, right now it is voluntary in many communities. *Those of us who participate in recycling are amazed by how much material is recycled.* **For many communities, the blue-box recycling program has had an immediate effect.** *By just recycling glass, aluminum cans, and plastic bottles, we have reduced the volume of disposable trash by one third, thus extending the useful life of local landfills by over a decade. Imagine the difference if those dramatic results were achieved nationwide.* **The amount of reusable items we thoughtlessly dispose of is staggering.** *For example, Americans dispose of enough steel everyday to supply Detroit car manufacturers for three months. Additionally, we dispose of enough aluminum annually to rebuild the nation's air fleet. These statistics, available from the Environmental Protection Agency (EPA), should encourage all of us to watch what we throw away.* **Clearly, recycling in our homes and in our communities directly improves the environment.**

Notice how the author's supporting examples enhance the message of the paragraph and relate to the author's thesis noted above. If you only read the bold-face sentences, you have a glimpse at the topic. This paragraph of, illustration, however, is developed through numerous details creating specific images: *reduced the volume of disposable trash by one-third; extended the useful life of local landfills by over a decade; enough steel everyday to supply Detroit car manufacturers for three months; enough aluminum to rebuild the nation's air fleet.* If the writer had merely written a few general sentences, as those shown in bold face, you would not fully understand the vast amount of trash involved in recycling or the positive results of current recycling efforts.

Skill 10.3   Determine meaning of words in context

Context clues help readers determine the meaning of words they are not familiar with. The context of a word is the sentence or sentences that surround the word.

Read the following sentences and attempt to determine the meanings of the words in bold print.

> The **luminosity** of the room was so incredible that there was no need for lights.
>
>> If there was no need for lights then one must assume that the word luminosity has something to do with giving off light. The definition of luminosity is: the emission of light.

Jamie could not understand Joe's feelings. His mood swings made understanding him somewhat of an **enigma.**

The fact that he could not be understood made him somewhat of a puzzle. The definition of enigma is: a mystery or puzzle.

Familiarity with word roots (the basic elements of words) and with prefixes can also help one determine the meanings of unknown words.

Following is a partial list of roots and prefixes. It might be useful to review these.

Root	Meaning	Example
aqua	water	aqualung
astro	stars	astrology
bio	life	biology
carn	meat	carnivorous
circum	around	circumnavigate
geo	earth	geology
herb	plant	herbivorous
mal	bad	malicious
neo	new	neonatal
tele	distant	telescope

Prefix	Meaning	Example
un-	not	unnamed
re-	again	reenter
il-	not	illegible
pre-	before	preset
mis-	incorrectly	misstate
in-	not	informal
anti-	against	antiwar
de-	opposite	derail
post-	after	postwar
ir-	not	irresponsible

Word forms

Sometimes a very familiar word can appear as a different part of speech.

You may have heard that *fraud* involves a criminal misrepresentation, so when it appears as the adjective form *fraudulent* ("He was suspected of fraudulent activities") you can make an educated guess. You probably know that something out of date is *obsolete;* therefore, when you read about "built-in *obsolescence,*" you can detect the meaning of the unfamiliar word.

TEACHER CERTIFICATION STUDY GUIDE

Practice questions: Read the following sentences and attempt to determine the meanings of the underlined words.

1. Farmer John got a two-horse plow and went to work. Straight <u>furrows</u> stretched out behind him.

   The word <u>furrows</u> means

   (A) long cuts made by plow
   (B) vast, open fields
   (C) rows of corn
   (D) pairs of hitched horses

2. The survivors struggled ahead, <u>shambling</u> through the terrible cold, doing their best not to fall.

   The word <u>shambling</u> means

   (A) frozen in place
   (B) running
   (C) shivering uncontrollably
   (D) walking awkwardly

Answers:

1. (A) is the correct answer. The words "straight" and the expression "stretched out behind him" are your clues.

2. (D) is the correct answer. The words "ahead" and "through" are your clues.

The context for a word is the written passage that surrounds it. Sometimes the writer offers synonyms—words that have nearly the same meaning. Context clues can appear within the sentence itself, within the preceding and/or following sentence(s), or in the passage as a whole.

Sentence clues

Often, a writer will actually **define** a difficult or particularly important word for you the first time it appears in a passage. Phrases like *that is, such as, which is,* or *is called* might announce the writer's intention to give just the definition you need. Occasionally, a writer will simply use a synonym (a word that means the same thing) or near-synonym joined by the word *or.* Look at the following examples:

> The credibility, that is to say the believability, of the witness was called into question by evidence of previous perjury.
> Nothing would assuage or lessen the child's grief.

Punctuation at the sentence level is often a clue to the meaning of a word. Commas, parentheses, quotation marks and dashes tell the reader that a definition is being offered by the writer.

> A tendency toward hyperbole, extravagant exaggeration, is a common flaw among persuasive writers.

> Political apathy - lack of interest - can lead to the death of the state.

A writer might simply give an **explanation** in other words that you can understand, in the same sentence:

> The xenophobic townspeople were suspicious of every foreigner.

Writers also explain a word in terms of its opposite at the sentence level:

> His incarceration was ended, and he was elated to be out of jail.

Adjacent sentence clues

The context for a word goes beyond the sentence in which it appears. At times, the writer uses adjacent (adjoining) sentences to present an explanation or definition:

> *The 200 dollars for the car repair would have to come out of the <u>contingency</u> fund. Fortunately, Angela's father had taught her to keep some money set aside for just such emergencies.*

Analysis: The second sentence offers a clue to the definition of *contingency* as used in this sentence: "emergencies." Therefore, a fund for contingencies would be money tucked away for unforeseen and/or urgent events.

Entire passage clues

On occasion, you must look at an entire paragraph or passage to figure out the definition of a word or term. In the following paragraph, notice how the word *nostalgia* undergoes a form of extended definition throughout the selection rather than in just one sentence.

> *The word <u>nostalgia</u> links Greek words for "away from home" and "pain." If you're feeling <u>nostalgic,</u> then, you are probably in some physical distress or discomfort, suffering from a feeling of alienation and separation from love ones or loved places. <u>Nostalgia</u> is that awful feeling you remember the first time you went away to camp or spent the weekend with a friend's family—homesickness, or some condition even more painful than that. But in common use, <u>nostalgia</u> has come to have more sentimental associations. A few years back, for example, a <u>nostalgia</u> craze had to do with the 1950s. We resurrected poodle skirts and saddle shoes, built new restaurants to look like old ones, and tried to make chicken a la king just as mother probably never made it. In TV situation comedies, we recreated a pleasant world that probably never existed and relished our <u>nostalgia,</u> longing for a homey, comfortable lost time.*

COMPETENCY 11.0 KNOWLEDGE OF INFERENTIAL COMPREHENSION

Skill 11.1 Determine purpose

An essay is an extended discussion of a writer's point of view about a particular topic. This point of view may be supported by using such writing modes as examples, argument and persuasion, analysis or comparison/contrast. in any case, a good essay is clear, coherent, well-organized and fully developed.

When an author sets out to write a passage, he/she usually has a purpose for doing so. That purpose may be to simply give information that might be interesting or useful to some reader or other; it may be to persuade the reader to a point of view or to move the reader to act in a particular way; it may be to tell a story; or it may be to describe something in such a way that an experience becomes available to the reader through one of the five senses. Following are the primary devices for expressing a particular purpose in a piece of writing:

- **Basic expository writing** simply gives information not previously known about a topic or is used to explain or define one. Facts, examples, statistics, cause and effect, direct tone, objective rather than subjective delivery, and non-emotional information are presented in a formal manner.

- **Descriptive writing** centers on person, place, or object, using concrete and sensory words to create a mood or impression and arranging details in a chronological or spatial sequence.

- **Narrative writing** is developed using an incident or anecdote or related series of events. Chronology, the 5 W's, topic sentence, and conclusion are essential ingredients.

- **Persuasive writing** implies the writer's ability to select vocabulary and arrange facts and opinions in such a way as to direct the actions of the listener/reader. Persuasive writing may incorporate exposition and narration as they illustrate the main idea.

- **Journalistic writing** is theoretically free of author bias. It is essential when relaying information about an event, person, or thing that it be factual and objective. Provide students with an opportunity to examine newspapers and create their own. Many newspapers have educational programs that are offered free to schools.

Tailoring language for a particular **audience** is an important skill. Writing to be read by a business associate will surely sound different from writing to be read by a younger sibling. Not only are the vocabularies different, but the formality/informality of the discourse will need to be adjusted.

The things to be aware of in determining what the language should be for a particular audience, then, hinges on two things: **word choice** and formality/informality. The most formal language does not use contractions or slang. The most informal language will probably feature a more casual use of common sayings and anecdotes. Formal language will use longer sentences and will not sound like a conversation. The most informal language will use shorter sentences—not necessarily simple sentences—but shorter constructions and may sound like a conversation.

In both formal and informal writing there exists a **tone**, the writer's attitude toward the material and/or readers. Tone may be playful, formal, intimate, angry, serious, ironic, outraged, baffled, tender, serene, or depressed, etc. The overall tone of a piece of writing is dictated by both the subject matter and the audience. Tone is also related to the actual words which make up the document, as we attach affective meanings to words, called **connotations**. Gaining this conscious control over language makes it possible to use language appropriately in various situations and to evaluate its uses in literature and other forms of communication. By evoking the proper responses from readers/listeners, we can prompt them to take action. The following questions are an excellent way to assess the audience and tone of a given piece of writing.

1. Who is your audience? (friend, teacher, business person, or someone else)
2. How much does this person know about you and/or your topic?
3. What is your purpose? (to prove an argument, to persuade, to amuse, to register a complaint, to ask for a raise, etc)
4. What emotions do you have about the topic? (nervous, happy, confident, angry, sad, no feelings at all)
5. What emotions do you want to register with your audience? (anger, nervousness, happiness, boredom, interest)
6. What persona do you need to create in order to achieve your purpose?
7. What choice of language is best suited to achieving your purpose with your particular subject? (slang, friendly but respectful, formal)
8. What emotional quality do you want to transmit to achieve your purpose (matter of fact, informative, authoritative, inquisitive, sympathetic, or angry) and to what degree do you want to express this tone?

Skill 11.2 Identify overall organizational pattern

The **organization** of a written work pertains to the order in which the writer has chosen to present the different parts of the discussion or argument and to the relationships he or she constructs among these parts.

Written ideas need to be presented in a **logical order** so that a reader can follow the information easily and quickly. There are many different ways in which to order a series of ideas, but they all share one thing in common: to lead the reader along a desired path in order to give a clear, strong presentation of the writer's main idea. These are some of the ways in which a paragraph may be organized:

Sequence of events – In this type of organization, the details are presented in the order in which they have occurred. Paragraphs that describe a process or procedure, give directions, or outline a given period of time (such as a day or a month) are often arranged chronologically.

Statement support – In this type of organization, the main idea is stated, and the rest of the paragraph explains or proves it. This is also referred to as order of relative importance. There are four ways in which this type of order is organized: most-to-least, least-to-most, most-least-most, and least-most-least.

Comparison-Contrast – In this type of organization, the compare-contrast pattern is used when a paragraph describes the differences or similarities of two or more ideas, actions, events, or things. Usually, the topic sentence describes the basic relationship between or among the ideas or items and the rest of the paragraph explains this relationship in more detail.

Classification – in this type of organization, the paragraph presents grouped information about a topic. The topic sentence usually states the general category, and the rest of the sentences show how and (to what extent) various elements of the category have a common base.

Cause and Effect – This pattern describes how two or more events are connected. The main sentence usually states the primary cause(s), the primary effect(s), and how they are basically connected. The rest of the sentences explain the connection in more detail.

Spatial/Place – In this type of organization, certain descriptions are organized according to the location of items in relation to each other and to a larger context. The orderly arrangement guides readers' eyes as they mentally envision the scene or place being described.

Example, Clarification, and Definition – These types of organizations show, explain, or elaborate on the main idea. This can be done by showing specific cases, by examining meaning multiple times, or by describing one item extensively.

Skill 11.3 Distinguish between fact and opinion

Facts are statements that are verifiable. Opinions are statements that must be supported in order to be accepted, such as beliefs, values, judgments, or feelings. Facts are objective information used to support subjective opinions. For example, "Jane is a bad girl" is an opinion. However, "Jane hit her sister with a baseball bat" is a *fact* upon which the opinion is based. Judgments are opinions—decisions or declarations based on observation or reasoning that express approval or disapproval. Facts report what has happened or exists and come from observation, measurement, or calculation. Facts can be tested and verified, whereas opinions and judgments cannot. They can only be supported with facts.

Most statements cannot be so clearly distinguished. "I believe that Jane is a bad girl" is a fact. The speaker knows what he or she believes. However, it obviously includes a judgment that could be disputed by another person who might believe otherwise. Judgments are not usually so firm. They are, rather, plausible opinions that provoke thought or lead to factual development.

Joe DiMaggio, a Yankees' center-fielder, was replaced by Mickey Mantle in 1952.

This is a fact. If necessary, evidence can be produced to support this.

First year players are more ambitious than seasoned players.
This is an opinion. There is no proof to support that everyone feels this way

Practice Questions: Decide if the statement is fact or opinion

1. The Inca were a group of Indians who ruled an empire in South America.

    (A) fact
    (B) opinion

2. The Inca were clever.

    (A) fact
    (B) opinion

Answers:

1. (A) is the correct answer. Research can prove this to be true.
2. (B) is the correct answer. It is doubtful that all people who have studied the Inca agree with this statement. Therefore, the proof is not conclusive.

Skill 11.4   Recognize bias

Bias is defined as an opinion, feeling or influence that strongly favors one side in an argument. A statement or passage is biased if an author attempts to convince a reader of something.

Is there evidence of bias in the following statement?

> *Using a calculator cannot help a student understand the process of graphing, so its use is a waste of time.*

Since the author makes it perfectly clear that he does not favor the use of the calculator in graphing problem, the answer is yes, there is evidence of bias. He has included his opinion in this statement.

Practice Question: Read the following paragraph and select an answer

> There are teachers who feel that computer programs are quite helpful in helping students grasp certain math concepts. There are also those who disagree with this feeling. It is up to each individual math teacher to decide if computer programs benefit her particular group of students.
>
> Is there evidence of bias in this paragraph?
> (A) yes
> (B) no

Answer: Since the author makes it perfectly clear that he does not favor the use of the calculator in graphing problem, the answer is (A). He has included his opinion in this statement.

Skill 11.5 Recognize tone

The **tone** of a written passage refers to an author's attitude toward the subject matter. The tone (mood, feeling) is revealed through such stylistic elements as vocabulary choice and sentence structure. The tone of the written passage is much like a speaker's voice; instead of being spoken, however, it is the product of words on a page.

Often, writers have an emotional stake in the subject; and their purpose, either explicitly or implicitly, is to convey those feelings to the reader. In such cases, the writing is generally subjective: that is, it stems from opinions, judgments, values, ideas, and feelings. Both sentence structure (syntax) and word choice (diction) are instrumental tools in creating tone.

Tone may be thought of generally as positive, negative, or neutral. Below is a statement about snakes that demonstrates this.

> *Many species of snakes live in Florida. Some of those species, both poisonous and non-poisonous, share habitats with humans.*

The voice of the writer in this statement is neutral. The sentences are declarative (not exclamations, fragments, or questions). The adjectives are few and nondescript—*many, some, poisonous* (balanced with *non-poisonous*). Nothing much in this brief paragraph would alert the reader to the feelings of the writer about snakes. The paragraph has a neutral, objective, detached, impartial tone.

If the writer's attitude toward snakes involves admiration or even affection, the tone would generally be positive:

> *Florida's snakes are a tenacious bunch. When they find their habitats invaded by humans, they cling to their home territories as long as they can, as if vainly attempting to fight off the onslaught of the human hordes.*

An additional message emerges in this paragraph: The writer quite clearly favors snakes over people. The writer uses positive adjectives like *tenacious* to describe the snakes. The writer also humanizes the reptiles, making them seem to be brave, beleaguered creatures. Obviously, the writer is more sympathetic to snakes than to people in this paragraph.

If the writer's attitude toward snakes involves active dislike and fear, then the tone would also reflect that attitude by being negative:

> *Countless species of snakes, some more dangerous than others, still lurk on the urban fringes of Florida's towns and cities. They will often invade domestic spaces, terrorizing people and their pets.*

Here, obviously, the snakes are the villains. They *lurk,* they *invade,* and they *terrorize.* The tone of this paragraph might be said to be distressed about snakes. In the same manner, a writer can use language to portray characters as good or bad. A writer uses positive and negative adjectives, as seen above, to express what a character is like.

Skill 11.6   Determine relationships between sentences

Most sentences cannot meaningfully stand alone. To read a passage without recognizing how each sentence is linked to those around it is to lose the passage's meaning. There are many ways in which sentences can be connected to one another:

Addition – one sentence is "tacked on" to another, without making one sentence depend upon the other. Both are equally important.

> *Joanna recently purchased a new stereo system, computer, and home alarm system. She **also** put down a payment on a new automobile.*

Clarification – One sentence restates the point of an earlier one, but in different terms.

> *The national debt is growing continually. **In fact**, by next year it may be five trillion dollars.*

Comparison/Contrast – Connection is one of similarity or difference.

> *Shelley's strained relationship with his father led the poet to a life of rebellion. **Likewise**, Byron's Bohemian lifestyle may be traced to his ambivalence towards authority.*

Example – One sentence works to make another more concrete or specific.

> *Sarah has always been an optimistic person. She believes that when she graduates from college she will get the job of her choice. (implicit)*

Location/Spatial Order – The relationship between sentences shows the placement of objects or items relative to each other in space.

The park was darkened by the school building's shadow. However, the sun still splashed the front window with light.(implicit)

Cause/Effect – One event (cause) brings about the second event (effect).

*General Hooker failed to anticipate General Lee's bold maneuver. **As a result**, Hooker's army was nearly routed by a smaller force.*

Summary – A summary sentence surveys and captures the most important points of the previous sentence(s).

*Every Fourth of July Ralph brings his whole family to the local parade, every Memorial Day he displays the flag, and every November fourth he votes. **On the whole**, he's a patriotic American.*

Skill 11.7 Analyze the validity of arguments

On the test, the terms **valid** and invalid have special meaning. If an argument is valid, it is reasonable. It is objective (not biased) and can be supported by evidence. If an argument is invalid, it is not reasonable. It is not objective. In other words, one can find evidence of bias.

Practice Questions: Read the following passages and select an answer.

1. Most dentists agree that Bright Smile Toothpaste is the best for fighting cavities. It tastes good and leaves your mouth minty fresh.

    Is this a valid or invalid argument?

    (A) valid
    (B) invalid

2. It is difficult to decide who will make the best presidential candidate, Senator Johnson or Senator Keeley. They have both been involved in scandals and have both gone through messy divorces while in office.

    Is this argument valid or invalid?

    (A) valid
    (B) invalid

Answers:

(A) is the correct choice. The author appears to be listing facts. He does not seem to favor one candidate over the other.

It is invalid (B). It mentions that "most" dentists agree. What about those who do not agree? The author is clearly exhibiting bias in leaving those who disagree out.

Skill 11.8 Draw logical inferences and conclusions

An **inference** is sometimes called an "educated guess" because it requires that you go beyond the strictly obvious to create additional meaning by taking the text one logical step further. Inferences and conclusions are based on the content of the passage – that is, on what the passage says or how the writer says it – and are derived by reasoning.

Inference is an essential and automatic component of most reading. For example, it is operative in determining the meaning of unknown words, the authors' main ideas, or whether or not authors have a bias. Such is the essence of inference: you use your own ability to reason in order to figure out what writers imply. As a reader, then, you must often logically extend your thinking in order to understand what authors only imply.

Consider the following example. Assume that you are an employer and that you are reading over the letters of reference submitted by a prospective employee for the position of clerk/typist in your real estate office. The position requires the applicant to be neat, careful, trustworthy, and punctual. You come across this letter of reference submitted by an applicant:

To whom it may concern,

Todd Finley has asked me to write a letter of reference for him. I am well qualified to do so because he worked for me for three months last year. His duties included answering the phone, greeting the public, and producing some simple memos and notices on the computer. Although Todd initially had few computer skills and little knowledge of telephone etiquette, he did acquire some during his stay with us. Todd's manner of speaking, both on the telephone and with the clients who came to my establishment, could be described as casual. He was particularly effective when communicating with peers. Please contact me by telephone if you wish to have further information about my experience.

TEACHER CERTIFICATION STUDY GUIDE

Here the writer implies, rather than openly states, the main idea. This letter calls attention to itself because there's a problem with its tone. A truly positive letter would say something like "I have distinct honor to recommend Todd Finley." Here, however, the letter simply verifies that Todd worked in the office. Second, the praise is obviously lukewarm. For example, the writer says that Todd "was particularly effective when communicating with peers." And educated guess translates that statement into a nice way of saying that Todd was not serious enough in his communications with clients.

In order to draw **inferences** and come to **conclusions**, a reader must use prior knowledge and apply it to the current situation. A conclusion is rarely, and an inference is never, stated. You must rely on your inferential skills to apprehend them.

Practice Questions: Read the following passages, and select an answer

1. Tim Sullivan had just turned 15. As a birthday present, his parents had given him a guitar and a certificate for 10 guitar lessons. He had always shown a love of music and a desire to learn an instrument. Tim began his lessons, and, before long, he was making up his own songs. At the music studio, Tim met Josh, who played the piano, and Roger, whose instrument was the saxophone. They all shared the same dream of starting a band, and each was praised by his teacher as having real talent.

   From this passage one can infer that

   A. Tim, Roger & Josh are going to start their own band.
   B. Tim is going to give up his guitar lessons.
   C. Tim, Josh & Roger will no longer be friends.
   D. Josh & Roger are going to start their own band.

2. The Smith family waited patiently around Carousel Number 7 for their luggage to arrive. They were exhausted after their 5-hour trip and were anxious to get to their hotel. After about an hour, they realized that they no longer recognized any of the other passengers' faces. Mrs. Smith asked the person who appeared to be in charge if they were at the right carousel. The man replied, "Yes, this is it, but we finished unloading that baggage almost half an hour ago."

   From the man's response we can infer that:

   A. The Smiths were ready to go to their hotel.
   B. The Smith's luggage was lost.
   C. The man had their luggage.
   D. They were at the wrong carousel.

GENERAL KNOWLEDGE

Answers:

1. (A) is the correct choice. Given the facts that Tim wanted to be a musician and start his own band, after meeting others who shared the same dreams, Tim probably joined them in an attempt to make their dreams become reality.

2. Since the Smiths were still waiting for their luggage, we know that they were not yet ready to go to their hotel. From the man's response, we know that they were not at the wrong carousel and that he did not have their luggage. Therefore, though not directly stated, it appears that their luggage was lost. Choice (B) is the correct answer.

In developing a line of reasoning, writers choose either inductive, going from the specific to the general, or deductive, going from the general to the specific. Inductive reasoning is suggested by the following sentences: "I tasted a green apple from my grandfather's yard when I was five years old, and it was sour. I also tasted a green apple that my friend brought to school in his lunchbox when I was eight years old, and it was sour. I was in Browns' Roadside Market and bought some green Granny Smith apples last week, and they were sour." This is a series of specifics. From those specifics, I might draw a conclusion—a generalization—all apples are sour, and I would have reasoned inductively to arrive at that generalization.

The same simplistic argument developed deductively would begin with the generalization that all green apples are sour. Then specifics would be offered to support that generalization: the sour green apple I tasted in my grandfather's orchard, the sour green apple in my friend's lunchbox, and the Granny Smith apples from the market.

When reasoning is this simple and straightforward, it's easy to follow, but it's also easy to see fallacies. For example, this person hasn't tasted all the green apples in the world; and, in fact, some green apples are not sour. However, it's rarely that easy to see the generalizations and the specifics. In determining whether a point has been proven, it's necessary to do that.

Sometimes generalizations are cited on the assumption that they are commonly accepted and do not need to be supported. An example: all men die sooner or later. Examples wouldn't be needed because that is commonly accepted. Now, some people might require that "die" be defined, but even the definition of "die" is assumed in this generalization.

Here are some current generalizations that may command common acceptance: providing healthcare for all citizens is the responsibility of the government; all true patriots will support any war the government declares.

Sample Test: Reading

Read the following paragraph, and answer the questions that follow.

    This writer has often been asked to tutor hospitalized children with cystic fibrosis. While undergoing all the precautionary measures to see these children (i.e. scrubbing thoroughly and donning sterilized protective gear- for the children's protection), she has often wondered why their parents subject these children to the pressures of schooling and trying to catch up on what they have missed because of hospitalization, a normal part of cystic fibrosis patients' lives. These children undergo so many tortuous treatments a day that it seems cruel to expect them to learn as normal children do, especially with their life expectancies being as short as they are.

1. What is meant by the word "precautionary" in the second sentence?

 A. Careful
 B. Protective
 C. Medical
 D. Sterilizing

2. What is the main idea of this passage?

 A. There is a lot of preparation involved in visiting a patient of cystic fibrosis.
 B. Children with cystic fibrosis are incapable of living normal lives.
 C. Certain concessions should be made for children with cystic fibrosis.
 D. Children with cystic fibrosis die young.

3. What is the author's tone?

 A. Sympathetic
 B. Cruel
 C. Disbelieving
 D. Cheerful

4. How is the author so familiar with the procedures used when visiting a child with cystic fibrosis?

 A. She has read about it.
 B. She works in a hospital.
 C. She is the parent of one.
 D. She often tutors them.

5. What is the author's purpose?

 A. To inform
 B. To entertain
 C. To describe
 D. To narrate

6. **What type of organizational pattern is the author using?**

   A. Classification
   B. Explanation
   C. Comparison and contrast
   D. Cause and effect

7. **The author states that it is "cruel" to expect children with cystic fibrosis to learn as "normal" children do. Is this a fact or an opinion?**

   A. Fact
   B. Opinion

8. **Is there evidence of bias in this paragraph?**

   A. Yes
   B. No

9. **What kind of relationship is found within the last sentence which starts with "These children undergo..." and ends with "...as short as they are"?**

   A. Addition
   B. Explanation
   C. Generalization
   D. Classification

10. **Does the author present an argument that is valid or invalid concerning the schooling of children with cystic fibrosis?**

    A. Valid
    B. Invalid

Read the following passage, and answer the questions that follow.

Disciplinary practices have been found to affect diverse areas of child development such as moral values, obedience to authority, and performance at school. Even though the dictionary has a specific definition for the word "discipline," it is still open to interpretation by people of different cultures.

There are four types of disciplinary styles: assertion of power, withdrawal of love, reasoning, and permissiveness. Assertion of power involves the use of force to discourage unwanted behavior. Withdrawal of love involves making the love of a parent conditional on children's good behavior. Reasoning involves persuading children to behave one way rather than another. Permissiveness involves allowing children to do as they please and face the consequences of their actions.

11. **What is the meaning of the word "diverse" in the first sentence?**

    A. Many
    B. Related to children
    C. Disciplinary
    D. M

12. Name the four types of disciplinary styles.

    A. Reasoning, power assertion, morality, and permissiveness.
    B. Morality, reasoning, permissiveness, and withdrawal of love.
    C. Withdrawal of love, permissiveness, assertion of power, and reasoning.
    D. Permissiveness, morality, reasoning, and power assertion.

13. What organizational structure is used in the first sentence of the second paragraph?

    A. Addition
    B. Explanation
    C. Definition
    D. Simple listing

14. What is the main idea of this passage?

    A. Different people have different ideas of what discipline is.
    B. Permissiveness is the most widely used disciplinary style.
    C. Most people agree on their definition of discipline.
    D. There are four disciplinary styles.

15. What is the author's purpose in writing this?

    A. To describe
    B. To narrate
    C. To entertain
    D. To inform

16. Is this passage biased?

    A. Yes
    B. No

17. What is the author's tone?

    A. Disbelieving
    B. Angry
    C. Informative
    D. Optimistic

18. What is the overall organizational pattern of this passage?

    A. Generalization
    B. Cause and effect
    C. Addition
    D. Summary

19. The author states that "assertion of power involves the use of force to discourage unwanted behavior." Is this a fact or an opinion?

    A. Fact
    B. Opinion

20. **From reading this passage we can conclude that**

    A. The author is a teacher.
    B. The author has many children.
    C. The author has written a book about discipline.
    D. The author has done a lot of research on discipline.

21. **What does the technique of reasoning involve?**

    A. Persuading children to behave in a certain way.
    B. Allowing children to do as he/she pleases.
    C. Using force to discourage unwanted behavior.
    D. Making love conditional on good behavior.

Read the following passage, and answer the questions that follow.

One of the most difficult problems plaguing American education is the assessment of teachers. No one denies that teachers ought to be answerable for what they do, but what exactly does that mean? The Oxford American Dictionary defines accountability as the obligation to give a reckoning or explanation for one's actions.

Do students have to learn for teaching to have taken place? Historically, teaching has not been defined in this restrictive manner; teachers were thought to be responsible for the quantity and quality of material covered and for the way in which it was presented. However, some definitions of teaching now imply that students must learn in order for teaching to have taken place.

As a teacher who tries my best to keep current on all the latest teaching strategies, I believe that those teachers who do not bother even to pick up an educational journal every once in a while should be kept under close watch. There are many teachers out there who have been teaching for decades and refuse to change their ways even if research has proven that their methods are outdated and ineffective. There is no place in the profession of teaching for these types of individuals. It is time that the American educational system clean house, for the sake of our children.

22. **What is the meaning of the word "reckoning" in the third sentence?**

    A. Thought
    B. Answer
    C. Obligation
    D. Explanation

23. **What is the organizational pattern of the second paragraph?**

    A. Cause and effect
    B. Classification
    C. Addition
    D. Explanation

24. What is the main idea of the passage?

    A. Teachers should not be answerable for what they do.
    B. Teachers who do not do their job should be fired.
    C. The author is a good teacher.
    D. Assessment of teachers is a serious problem in society today.

25. Is this a valid argument?

    A. Yes
    B. No

26. From the passage, one can infer that

    A. The author considers herself a good teacher.
    B. Poor teachers will be fired.
    C. Students have to learn for teaching to take place.
    D. The author will be fired.

27. Teachers who do not keep current on educational trends should be fired. Is this a fact or an opinion?

    A. Fact
    B. Opinion

28. The author states that teacher assessment is a problem for

    A. Elementary schools
    B. Secondary schools
    C. American education
    D. Families

29. What is the author's purpose in writing this?

    A. To entertain
    B. To narrate
    C. To describe
    D. To persuade

30. Is there evidence of bias in this passage?

    A. Yes
    B. No

31. What is the author's overall organizational pattern?

    A. Classification
    B. Cause and effect
    C. Definition
    D. Comparison and contrast

32. The author's tone is one of

    A. Disbelief
    B. Excitement
    C. Support
    D. Concern

33. **What is meant by the word "plaguing" in the first sentence?**

    A. Causing problems
    B. Causing illness
    C. Causing anger
    D. Causing failure

34. **Where does the author get her definition of "accountability?"**

    A. Webster's Dictionary
    B. Encyclopedia Brittanica
    C. Oxford Dictionary
    D. World Book Encyclopedia

Read the following paragraph, and answer the questions that follow.

Mr. Smith gave instructions for the painting to be hung on the wall. And then it leaped forth before his eyes: the little cottages on the river, the white clouds floating over the valley, and the green of the towering mountain ranges which were seen in the distance. The painting was so vivid that it seemed almost real. Mr. Smith was now absolutely certain that the painting had been worth money.

35. **What does the author mean by the expression "it leaped forth before his eyes"?**

    A. The painting fell off the wall.
    B. The painting appeared so real it was almost three-dimensional.
    C. The painting struck Mr. Smith in the face.
    D. Mr. Smith was hallucinating.

36. **From the last sentence, one can infer that**

    A. The painting was expensive.
    B. The painting was cheap.
    C. Mr. Smith was considering purchasing the painting.
    D. Mr. Smith thought the painting was too expensive and decided not to purchase it.

37. **What is the main idea of this passage?**

    A. The painting that Mr. Smith purchased is expensive.
    B. Mr. Smith purchased a painting.
    C. Mr. Smith was pleased with the quality of the painting he had purchased.
    D. The painting depicted cottages and valleys.

38. **The author's purpose is to**

    A. Inform
    B. Entertain
    C. Persuade
    D. Narrate

39. **What is the meaning of the word "vivid" in the third sentence?**

    A. Lifelike
    B. Dark
    C. Expensive
    D. Big

40. **Is this passage biased?**

    A. Yes
    B. No

Answer Key: Reading

1. B
2. C
3. A
4. S
5. C
6. B
7. B
8. A
9. B
10. B
11. A
12. C
13. D
14. A
15. D
16. B
17. C
18. C
19. A
20. D
21. A
22. D
23. D
24. D
25. B
26. A
27. B
28. C
29. D
30. A
31. C
32. D
33. A
34. C
35. B
36. A
37. C
38. D
39. A
40. B

TEACHER CERTIFICATION STUDY GUIDE

Rationales for Sample Questions: Reading

1. The correct answer is B. The writer uses expressions such as "protective gear" and "child's protection" to emphasize this.

2. The correct answer is C. The author states that she wonders "why parents subject these children to the pressures of schooling," and that "it seems cruel to expect them to learn as normal children do." In making these statements, she appears to be expressing the belief that these children should not have to do what "normal" children do. They have enough to deal with – their illness itself.

3. The correct answer is A. The author states that "it seems cruel to expect them to learn as normal children do," thereby indicating that she feels sorry for them.

4. The correct answer is D. The writer states this fact in the opening sentence.

5. The correct answer is C. The author is simply describing her experience in working with children with cystic fibrosis.

6. The correct answer is B. The author mentions tutoring children with cystic fibrosis in her opening sentence and goes on to "explain" some of these issues that are involved with her job.

7. The correct answer is B. The fact that she states that it "seems" cruel indicates that there is no evidence to support this belief.

8. The correct answer is A. The writer clearly feels sorry for these children and gears her writing in that direction.

9. The correct answer is B. In mentioning the their life expectancies are short, she is explaining by giving one reason why it is cruel to expect them to learn as normal children do.

10. The correct answer is B. Even though to most readers, the writer's argument makes good sense, it is biased and lacks real evidence.

11. The correct answer is A. Any of the other choices would be redundant in this sentence.

12. The correct answer is C. This is directly stated in the second paragraph.

13. The correct answer is D. The author simply states the types of disciplinary styles.

14. The correct answer is A. Choice C is not true; the opposite is stated in the passage. Choice B could be true, but we have no evidence of this. Choice D is just one of the many facts listed in the passage.

15. The correct answer is D. The author is providing the reader with information about disciplinary practices.

16. The correct answer is B. If the reader were so inclined, he could research discipline and find this information.

17. The correct answer is C. The author appears to simply be stating the facts.

18. The correct answer is C. The author has taken a subject, in this case discipline, and developed it point by point.

19. The correct answer is A. The author appears to have done extensive research on this subject.

20. The correct answer is D. Given all the facts mentioned in the passage, this is the only inference one can make.

21. The correct answer is A. This fact is directly stated in the second paragraph.

22. The correct answer is D. The meaning of this word is directly stated in the same sentence.

23. The correct answer is D. The author goes on to further explain what she meant by"...what exactly does that mean?" in the first paragraph.

24. The correct answer is D. Most of the passage is dedicated to elaborating on why teacher assessment is such a problem.

25. The correct answer is B. In the third paragraph, the author appears to be resentful of lazy teachers.

26. The correct answer is A. The first sentence of the third paragraph alludes to this.

27. The correct answer is B. There may be those who feel they can be good teachers by using old methods.

28. The correct answer is C. This fact is directly stated in the first paragraph.

29. The correct answer is D. The author does some describing, but the majority of her statements seemed geared towards convincing the reader that teachers who are lazy or who do not keep current should be fired.

TEACHER CERTIFICATION STUDY GUIDE

30. The correct answer A. The entire third paragraph is the author's opinion on the matter.

31. The correct answer is C. The author identifies teacher assessment as a problem and spends the rest of the passage defining why it is considered a problem.

32. The correct answer is D. The author appears concerned with the future of education.

33. The correct answer is A. The first paragraph makes this definition clear.

34. The correct answer is C. This is directly stated in the third sentence of the first paragraph.

35. The correct answer is B. This is almost directly stated in the third sentence.

36. The correct answer is A. Choice B is incorrect because, had the painting been cheap, chances are that Mr. Smith would no have considered his purchase. Choices C and D are ruled out by the fact that the painting had already been purchased. The author makes this clear when she says, "...the painting had been worth the money."

37. The correct answer is C. Every sentence in the paragraph alludes to this fact.

38. The correct answer is D. The author is simply narrating or telling the story of Mr. Smith and his painting.

39. The correct answer is A. This is reinforced by the second half of the same sentence.

40. The correct answer is B. The author appears merely to be telling what happened when Mr. Smith had his new painting hung on the wall.

GENERAL KNOWLEDGE

DOMAIN IV.   ESSAY

The General Knowledge Essay subtest requires that the examinee select from two topics and organize and compose an original essay in 50 minutes. The intent of the essay test component is to show that you can, in the time allotted, compose and write an original essay that completely addresses the topic in an effective, well-organized manner with good grammar and spelling. An examinee is absolutely not permitted to memorize an essay from another source and present it as an original essay. Doing so is considered cheating, and if the essay is identified as being pre-prepared, all tests taken that day will be invalidated, and no scores will be received. In addition, the incident will be reported to the Department's Bureau of Professional Practices Services.

GENERAL STRATEGIES FOR WRITING THE ESSAY

1. Watch the time.	Use *all* the time wisely. You shouldn't run out of time before you are done; nor should you write an incomplete essay because you didn't use all the time allowed.
2. Read the instructions carefully, and select one of the topics.	Determine what the topic is asking. Think of how the topic relates to what you know, what you have learned, and what experiences you have had so that you can provide concrete details rather than vague generalities.
3. Take a few minutes to prewrite.	Jot down your first ideas. Sketch a quick outline or group your ideas together with arrows or numbers.
4. Write a thesis statement that provides a clear focus for your essay.	In your thesis, state a point of view that guides the purpose and scope of your essay. Consider the larger point you're trying to convey to the reader and what you want the reader to understand about the topic. Avoid a thesis statement framed as a fact statement, a question, or an announcement.
5. Develop the essay considering your purpose.	Develop paragraphs fully; give examples and reasons that support your thesis. Indent each new paragraph. Note that a good essay may be longer or shorter than the basic five-paragraph format of some short essays. The key is to **develop** a topic by using concrete, informative details.
6. Tie your main ideas together with a brief conclusion.	Provide a concluding paragraph that ties together the essay's points and offers insights about the topic. Avoid a conclusion that merely restates the thesis and repeats the supporting details.
7. Revise/proofread the essay so that it conforms to standard American English.	Look for particular errors you tend to make. Mark errors, and correct them. You'll never be penalized for clearly crossing out errors. Look for words, sentences, or even paragraphs that need changing. Write legibly so that the reader knows what you have written.

Skill 12.1 Determine the purpose for writing

Topic Analysis

Even before you select a topic, determine what each prompt is asking you to discuss. This first decision is crucial. If you pick a topic that you don't really understand or about which you have little to say, you'll have difficulty developing your essay. So take a few moments to analyze each topic carefully *before* you begin to write.

Topic A: A modern invention that can be considered a wonder of the world

In general, the topic prompts have two parts:

> the *SUBJECT* of the topic and
> an *ASSERTION* about the subject.

The **subject** is *a modern invention*. In this prompt, the word *modern* indicates you should discuss something invented recently, at least in this century. The word *invention* indicated you're to write about something created by humans (not natural phenomena such as mountains or volcanoes). You may discuss an invention that has potential for harm, such as chemical warfare or the atomic bomb or you may discuss an invention that has the potential for good: the computer, DNA testing, television, antibiotics, and so on.

The **assertion** (a statement of point of view) is that *the invention has such powerful or amazing qualities that it should be considered a wonder of the world*. The assertion states your point of view about the subject, and it limits the range for discussion. In other words, you would discuss particular qualities or uses of the invention, not just discuss how it was invented or whether it should have been invented at all.

Note also that this particular topic encourages you to use examples to show the reader that a particular invention is a modern wonder. Some topic prompts lend themselves to essays with an argumentative edge, one in which you take a stand on a particular issue and persuasively prove your point. Here, you undoubtedly could offer examples or illustrations of the many "wonders" and uses of the particular invention you chose.

Be aware that misreading or misinterpreting the topic prompt can lead to serious problems. Papers that do not address the topic occur when one reads too quickly or only half-understands the topic. This may happen if you misread or misinterpret words. Misreading can also lead to a paper that addresses only part of the topic prompt rather than the entire topic.

See also Skill 11.1

Skill 12.2 Formulate a thesis or statement of main idea

To develop a complete essay, spend a few minutes planning. Jot down your ideas, and quickly sketch an outline. Although you may feel under pressure to begin writing, you will write more effectively if you plan out your major points.

Prewriting
Before actually writing, you'll need to generate content and to develop a writing plan. Three prewriting techniques that can be helpful are:

Brainstorming

When brainstorming, quickly create a list of words and ideas that are connected to the topic. Let your mind roam freely to generate as many relevant ideas as possible in a few minutes. For example, on the topic of computers you may write:

> computer- modern invention
> types- personal computers, micro-chips in calculators and watches
> wonder - acts like an electronic brain
> uses - science, medicine, offices, homes, schools
> problems- too much reliance; the machines aren't perfect

This list could help you focus on the topic and states the points you could develop in the body paragraphs. The brainstorming list keeps you on track and is well worth the few minutes it takes to jot down the ideas. While you haven't ordered the ideas, seeing them on paper is an important step.

Questioning

Questioning helps you focus as you mentally ask a series of exploratory questions about the topic. You may use the most basic questions: **who, what, where, when, why, and how.**

"**What** is my subject? "
> [computers]

"**What** types of computers are there?"
> [personal computers, micro-chip computers]

"**Why** have computers been a positive invention?"
> [act like electronic brains in machinery and equipment; help solve complex scientific problems]

"How have computers been a positive invention?"
[used to make improvements in:
- science (space exploration, moon landings)
- medicine (MRIs, CAT scans, surgical tools, research models)
- business (PCs, FAX, telephone equipment)
- education (computer programs for math, languages, science, social studies), and
- personal use (family budgets, tax programs, healthy diet plans)

"How can I show that computers are good?"
[citing numerous examples]

"What problems do I see with computers?"
[too much reliance; not yet perfect.]

"What personal experiences would help me develop examples to respond to this topic?
[my own experiences using computers]

Of course, you may not have time to write out the questions completely. You might just write the words *who, what, where, why, how* and the major points next to each. An abbreviated list might look as follows:

What — computers/modern wonder/making life better
How — through technological improvements: lasers, calculators, CAT scans, MRIs.

Where – in science and space exploration, medicine, schools, offices

In a few moments, your questions should help you to focus on the topic and to generate interesting ideas and points to make in the essay. Later in the writing process, you can look back at the list to be sure that you've made the key points you intended.

Clustering

Some visual thinkers find clustering an effective prewriting method. When clustering, you draw a box in the center of your paper and write your topic within that box. Then you draw lines from the center box and connect it to small satellite boxes that contain related ideas. Note the cluster on the next page:

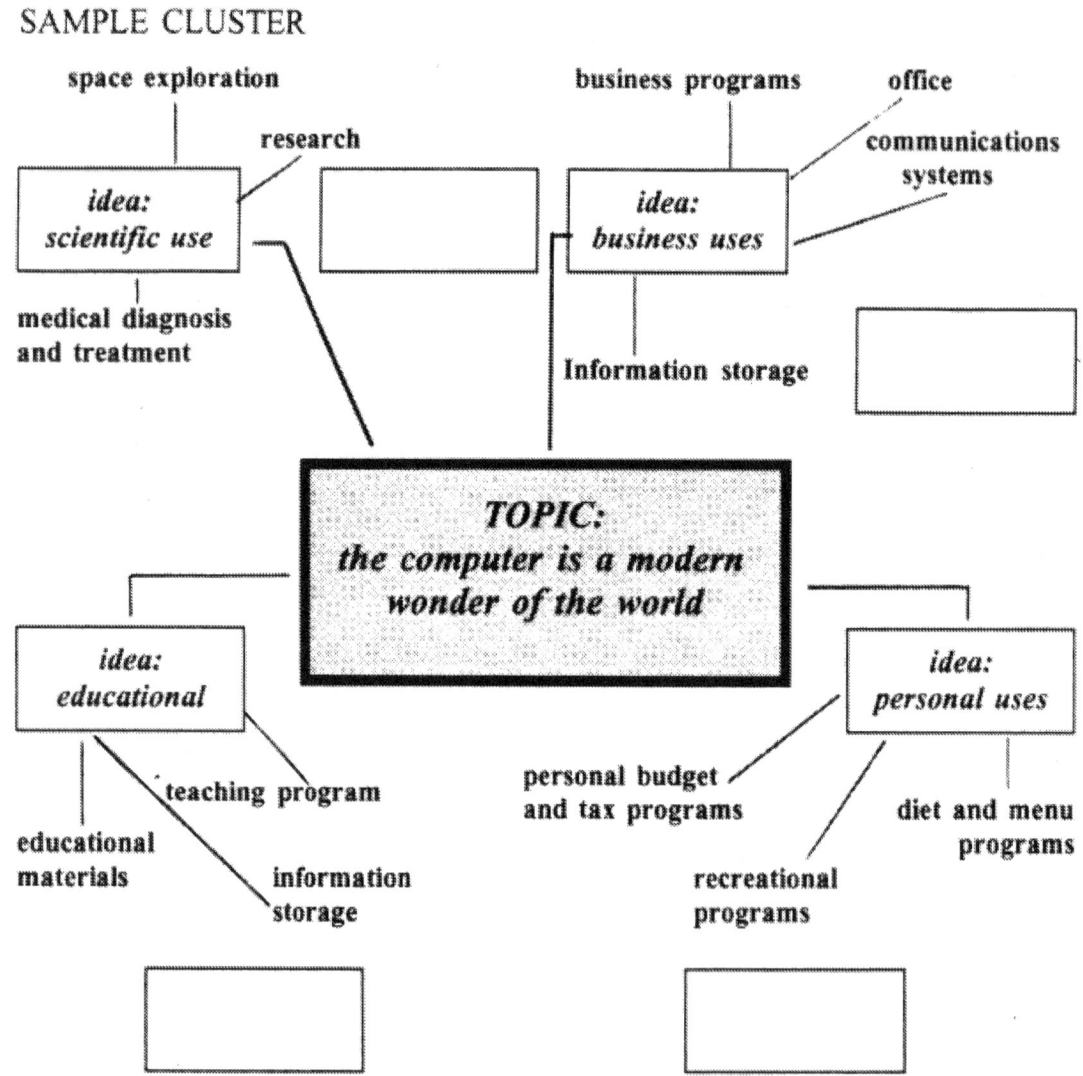

Writing the Thesis

After focusing on the topic and generating your ideas, form your thesis, the controlling idea of your essay. The thesis is your general statement to the reader expressing your point of view and guiding your essay's purpose and scope. The thesis should allow you either to explain your subject or to take an arguable position about it. A strong thesis statement is neither too narrow nor too broad.

Subject and Assertion of the Thesis

From the analysis of the general topic, you saw the topic in terms of its two parts - *subject* and *assertion*. On the exam, your thesis or viewpoint on a particular topic states two important points:

1. the *SUBJECT* of the paper
2. the *ASSERTION* about the subject.

The **subject of the thesis** relates directly to the topic prompt, but expresses the specific area you have chosen to discuss. (Remember that the exam topic will be general and will allow you to choose a particular subject related to the topic). For example, the computer is one modern invention.

The **assertion of the thesis** is your viewpoint, or opinion, about the subject. The assertion provides the motive or purpose for your essay, and it may be an arguable point or one that explains or illustrates a point of view.

For example, you may present an argument for or against a particular issue. You may contrast two people, objects, or methods to show that one is better than the other. You may analyze a situation in all aspects and make recommendations for improvement. You may assert that a law or policy should be adopted, changed, or abandoned. You may also, as in the computer example, explain to your reader that a situation or condition exists; rather than argue a viewpoint, you would use examples to illustrate your assertion about the essay's subject.

Specifically, the **subject** of Topic A is *the computer*. The **assertion** is that *it is a modern wonder that has improved our lives and that we rely on*. Now you quickly have created a workable thesis in a few moments:

> *The computer is a modern wonder of the world that has improved our lives and that we have come to rely on.*

Guidelines for Writing Thesis Statements

The following guidelines are not a formula for writing thesis statements; rather, they are general strategies for making your thesis statement clearer and more effective.

1. State a *particular point* of *view* about the topic with both a *subject* and an *assertion.* The thesis should give the essay purpose and scope and thus provide readers a guide. If the thesis is vague, your essay may be undeveloped because you do not have an idea to assert or a point to explain. Weak thesis statements are often framed as facts, questions, or announcements:

    a. Avoid a fact statement as a thesis. While a fact statement may provide a subject, it generally does not include a point of view about the subject that provides the basis for an extended discussion. Example: *Recycling saved our community over $10,000 last year.* This fact statement provides a detail, *not* a point of view. Such a detail might be found within an essay, but it does not state a point of view.

    b. Avoid framing the thesis as a vague question. In many cases, rhetorical questions do not provide a clear point of view for an extended essay. Example: *How do people recycle?* This question neither asserts a point of view nor helpfully guides the reader to understand the essay's purpose and scope.

    c. Avoid the "announcer" topic sentence that merely states the topic you will discuss
    Example: I *will discuss ways to recycle.* This sentence states the subject, but the scope of the essay is only suggested. Again, this statement does not assert a viewpoint that guides the essay's purpose. It merely "announces" that the writer will write about the topic.

2. Start with a workable thesis. You might revise your thesis as you begin writing and discover your own point of view.

3. If feasible and appropriate, perhaps state the thesis in multi-point form, expressing the scope of the essay. By stating the points in parallel form, you clearly lay out the essay's plan for the reader.
Example: *To improve the environment, we can recycle our trash, elect politicians who see the environment as a priority, and support lobbying groups who work for environmental protection.*

4. Because of the exam time limit, place your thesis in the first paragraph to key the reader to the essay's main idea.

Skill 12.3 Organize ideas and details effectively

Creating a working outline

A good thesis gives structure to your essay and helps focus your thoughts. When forming your thesis, look at your prewriting strategy – clustering, questioning, or brainstorming. Then decide quickly which two or three major areas you'll discuss. Remember you must limit *the scope* of the paper because of the time factor.

The **outline** lists those main areas or points as topics for each paragraph. Looking at the prewriting cluster on computers, you might choose several areas in which computers help us, for example in science and medicine, business, and education. You might also consider people's reliance on this "wonder" and include at least one paragraph about this reliance. A formal outline for this essay might look like the one below:

I. Introduction and thesis
II. Computers used in science and medicine
II. Computers used in business
IV. Computers used in education
V. People's reliance on computers
VI. Conclusion

Under time pressure, however, you may use a shorter organizational plan, such as abbreviated key words in a list. For example

1. intro: wonders of the computer OR
2. science
3. med
4. schools
5. business
6. conclusion

a. intro: wonders of computers - science
b. in the space industry
c. in medical technology
d. conclusion

Developing the essay

With a working thesis and outline, you can begin writing the essay. The essay should be in three main sections:

1) The **introduction** sets up the essay and leads to the thesis statement.
2) The **body paragraphs** are developed with concrete information leading from the **topic sentences**.
3) The **conclusion** ties the essay together.

Introduction

Put your thesis statement into a clear, coherent opening paragraph. One effective device is to use a funnel approach in which you begin with a brief description of the broader issue and then move to a clearly focused, specific thesis statement.

Consider the following introductions to the essay on computers. The length of each is an obvious difference. Read each and consider the other differences.
  Does each introduce the subject generally?
  Does each lead to a stated thesis?
  Does each relate to the topic prompt?

Introduction 1: *Computers are used every day. They have many uses. Some people who use them are workers, teachers, and doctors.*

Analysis: This introduction does give the general topic, computers used every day, but it does not explain what those uses are. This introduction does not offer a point of view in a clearly stated thesis, nor does it convey the idea that computers are a modem wonder.

Introduction 2: *Computers are used just about everywhere these days. I don't think there's an office around that doesn't use computers, and we use them a lot in all kinds of jobs. Computers are great for making life easier and work better. I don't think we'd get along without the computer.*

Analysis: This introduction gives the general topic about computers and mentions one area that uses computers. The thesis states that people couldn't get along without computers, but it does not state the specific areas that the essay discusses. Note, too, the meaning is not helped by vague diction such as *a lot* or *great*.

Introduction 3: *Each day, we either use computers or see them being used around us. We wake to the sound of a digital alarm operated by a micro-chip. Our cars run by computerized machinery. We use computers to help us learn. We receive phone calls and letters transferred from computers across continents. Our astronauts walked on the moon and returned safely because of computer technology. The computer, a wonderful electronic brain that we have come to rely on, has changed our world through advances in science, business, and education.*

Analysis: This introduction is the most thorough and fluent because it provides interest in the general topic and offers specific information about computers as a modern wonder. It also leads to a thesis that directs the reader to the scope of the discussion--advances in science, business, and education.

Topic Sentences

Just as the essay must have an overall focus reflected in the thesis statement, each paragraph must have a central idea reflected in the topic sentence. A good topic sentence also provides transition from the previous paragraph and relates to the essay's thesis. Good topic sentences, therefore, provide unity throughout the essay.

Consider the following potential topic sentences. Be sure that each provides transition and clearly states the subject of the paragraph.

Topic Sentence 1: *Computers are used in science.*

Analysis: This sentence simply states the topic--computers used in science. It does not relate to the thesis or provide transition from the introduction. The reader still does not know how computers are used.

Topic Sentence 2: *Now I will talk about computers used in science.*

Analysis: Like the faulty "announcer" thesis statement, this "announcer" topic sentence is vague and merely names the topic.

Topic Sentence 3: *First, computers used in science have improved our lives.*

Analysis: The transition word *First* helps link the introduction and this paragraph. It adds unity to the essay. It does not, however, give specifics about the improvement computers have made in our lives.

Topic Sentence 4: *First used in scientific research and spaceflights, computers are now used extensively in the diagnosis and treatment of disease.*

Analysis: This sentence is the most thorough and fluent. It provides specific areas that will be discussed in the paragraph and offers more than an announcement of the topic. The writer gives concrete information about the content of the paragraph that will follow.

Summary Guidelines for Writing Topic Sentences
1. Specifically relate the topic to the thesis statement.
2. State clearly and concretely the subject of the paragraph.
3. Provide some transition from the previous paragraph.
4. Avoid topic sentences that are facts, questions, or announcements.

Skill 12.4 Provide adequate, relevant supporting material

See Skill 10.2

Skill 12.5 Use effective transitions

See Skill 6.1

Skill 12.6 Demonstrate a mature command of language

See Competency 7.0

Skill 12.7 Avoid inappropriate use of slang, jargon and clichés

Slang is defined as "very informal usage in vocabulary and idiom that is characteristically more metaphorical, playful, elliptical, vivid, and ephemeral than ordinary language, as *Hit the road.* Slang is fine in conversation between friends, but it is extremely inappropriate in formal writing. Slang is oftentimes specific to a social group or geographic region. Because it is so colloquial, slang can be easily misunderstood. Moreover, using slang can affect how seriously readers regard your writing. The only time that slang may be appropriate in formal writing is when it is being used in a quote or dialogue.

Jargon is defined as "the language, esp. the vocabulary, peculiar to a particular trade, profession, or group: *medical jargon.*" Jargon pertains to the vocabulary use by a limited or specialized group of people. As a result, using jargon can affect clear and effective communication to a *general* reading public. Jargon, like slang, has its own time and place. If you are writing for a specialized audience, specialized language will communicate meaning effectively and show the audience that you are familiar with the terms associated with that specialized field. If, however, you are writing for a more general audience, jargon will be unintelligible gibberish and, perhaps, even offensive. If readers feel that an author is being pretentious or boastful, they may find the jargon distasteful.

A **cliché** is defined as "a trite, stereotyped expression; a sentence or phrase, usually expressing a popular or common thought or idea, that has lost originality, ingenuity, and impact by long overuse, as *sadder but wiser,* or *strong as an ox.*" The use of clichés weakens writing due to lack of creativity, thoughtfulness, and personal perspective. Clichés are boring and, sometimes, even offensive; and they are best to be avoided when one is writing an original work. Rather than using tired expressions to convey an idea, instead rethink the idea that is being conveyed, and reword it with correct vocabulary and specific details.

Skill 12.8 Use a variety of sentence patterns effectively

See Competency 8.0

Skill 12.9 Maintain consistent point of view

Point of view defines the focus a writer assumes in relation to a given topic. It is extremely important to maintain a consistent point of view in order to create coherent paragraphs. Point of view is related to matters of person, tense, tone, and number.

Person – A shift in the form which indicates whether a person is speaking (first), is being spoken to (second), or is being spoken about (third) can disrupt the continuity of a passage. In your essay, it is recommended that you write in the third person because it is often considered to be the most formal of the modes of person. If you do decide to use the more informal first or second person (I, you, we) in your essay, be careful not to shift between first, second, and third persons from sentence to sentence or paragraph to paragraph.

Tense – Verbs tenses indicate the time of an action or state of being – the past, present, or future. It is important, usually, to stick to a selected tense, though this may not always be the case. For instance, in an essay about the history of environmental protection, it might be necessary to include a paragraph about the future benefits or consequences of protecting Earth.

Tone – The tone of an essay varies greatly with the purpose, subject, and audience. It is best to assume a formal tone for this essay. (See Domain II, Skill 2.3).

Number – Words change when their meanings are singular or plural. Make sure that you do not shift number needlessly; if a meaning is singular in one sentence, do not make it plural in a subsequent sentence.

Skill 12.10 Observe the conventions of standard American English

See Domain II Competencies 6.0 – 9.0

XAMonline, INC. 21 Orient Ave. Melrose, MA 02176

Toll Free number 800-509-4128

TO ORDER Fax 781-662-9268 OR www.XAMonline.com

PROGRAM FOR LICENTURE FOR COLORADO EDUCATORS - PLACE - 2007

PO#   Store/School:

Address 1:

Address 2 (Ship to other):

City, State Zip

Credit card number_____-_____-_____-_____   expiration_____

EMAIL _____

PHONE   FAX

13# ISBN 2007	TITLE	Qty	Retail	Total
978-1-58197-705-9	PLACE ELEMENTARY EDUCATION 01			
978-1-58197-706-6	PLACE MATHEMATICS 04			
978-1-58197-707-3	PLACE SCIENCE 05			
978-1-58197-708-5	PLACE SOCIAL STUDIES 06			
978-1-58197-704-2	PLACE ENGLISH 07			
978-1-58197-709-7	PLACE FRENCH SAMPLE TEST 08			
978-1-58197-710-3	PLACE SPANISH 09			
978-1-58197-711-0	PLACE SPECIAL EDUCATION GENERALIST 20			
978-1-58197-712-7	PLACE ART SAMPLE TEST 28			
978-1-58197-713-4	PLACE PHYSICAL EDUCATION 32			
978-1-58197-702-8	PLACE FAMILY AND CONSUMER STUDIES 36			
978-1-58197-730-1	PLACE READING 18, 43			
978-1-58197-715-8	PLACE SCHOOL COUNSELOR 41			
978-1-58197-714-1	PLACE SCHOOL LIBRARY MEDIA 42			
978-1-58197-716-5	PLACE PRINCIPAL 80			
978-1-58197-768-4	PLACE BASIC SKILLS 90			
			SUBTOTAL	
	FOR PRODUCT PRICES GO TO WWW.XAMONLINE.COM		Ship	$8.25
			TOTAL	

www.ingramcontent.com/pod-product-compliance
Lightning Source LLC
Chambersburg PA
CBHW082037230426
43670CB00016B/2691